Schiller's *Wallenstein*, *Maria Stuart*, and *Die Jungfrau von Orleans*

Changing perceptions about history necessarily color the critical reception of historical plays, not only in terms of expectations regarding historical accuracy, but also in judgments about the value and suitability of historical material for the stage. The German playwright, poet, and philosopher Friedrich Schiller, often called the father of modern German drama, broke new ground with his late historical plays — the *Wallenstein* trilogy, *Maria Stuart*, and *Die Jungfrau von Orleans* — and they have thus generated a continuous stream of criticism since their appearance in the early nineteenth century. In this book Kathy Saranpa maps out three related strands: the reception history of Schiller's late historical plays; the changing view of history, from Herder's *Universalgeschichte* to the American New Historicism; and the changing status of the genre of the historical drama. The juxtaposition of these three strands will interest scholars of German literature; readers from other fields will appreciate the book's value as an introduction to the work of an often misunderstood but vastly important figure in German belles-lettres and philosophy.

Kathy Saranpa received her Ph.D. in Germanic languages and literatures from Yale University, and has taught at the universities of Wisconsin and Oregon.

Studies in German Literature, Linguistics, and Culture:
Literary Criticism in Perspective

Literary Criticism in Perspective

James Hardin (*South Carolina*), General Editor

Stephen D. Dowden (*Brandeis*), German Literature

Books in the series *Literary Criticism in Perspective* trace literary scholarship and criticism on major and neglected writers alike, or on a single major work, a group of writers, a literary school or movement. In so doing the authors — authorities on the topic in question who are also well-versed in the principles and history of literary criticism — address a readership consisting of scholars, students of literature at the graduate and undergraduate level, and the general reader. One of the primary purposes of the series is to illuminate the nature of literary criticism itself, to gauge the influence of social and historic currents on aesthetic judgments once thought objective and normative.

SCHILLER'S WALLENSTEIN, MARIA STUART, AND DIE JUNGFRAU VON ORLEANS

THE CRITICAL LEGACY

Kathy Saranpa

CAMDEN HOUSE

Copyright © 2002 Kathy J. Saranpa

All Rights Reserved. Except as permitted under current legislation,
no part of this work may be photocopied, stored in a retrieval system,
published, performed in public, adapted, broadcast, transmitted,
recorded, or reproduced in any form or by any means,
without the prior permission of the copyright owner.

First published 2002
by Camden House

Camden House is an imprint of Boydell & Brewer Inc.
PO Box 41026, Rochester, NY 14604–4126 USA
and of Boydell & Brewer Limited
PO Box 9, Woodbridge, Suffolk IP12 3DF, UK

ISBN: 1–57113–155–8

Library of Congress Cataloging-in-Publication Data

Saranpa, Kathy J. (Kathy Jo), 1955–
 Schiller's Wallenstein, Maria Stuart, and Die Jungfrau von Orleans: the critical legacy / Kathy J. Saranpa.
  p. cm. — (Studies in German literature, linguistics, and culture. Literary criticism in perspective)
 Includes bibliographical references and index.
 ISBN 1–57113–155–8 (alk. paper)
  1. Schiller, Friedrich, 1759–1805—Knowledge—History. 2. Historical drama, German—History and criticism. 3. Schiller, Friedrich, 1759–1805. Wallenstein. 4. Schiller, Friedrich, 1759–1805. Maria Stuart. 5. Schiller, Friedrich, 1759–1805. Jungfrau von Orleans. I. Title. II. Studies in German literature, linguistics, and culture (Unnumbered). Literary criticism in perspective.

PT2496.H5 S27 2002
832'.6—dc21

2001052670

A catalogue record for this title is available from the British Library.

This publication is printed on acid-free paper.
Printed in the United States of America.

To Erik

Contents

Acknowledgments — ix

Introduction — 1

1: The Legacy of the Enlightenment: Criticism by Schiller's Contemporaries — 13

2: Hegel, Herder, and Ranke: Schiller during the Century of Historicism — 33

3: The Metaphysical Crisis, the First World War, and the Aftermath — 67

4: Schiller's Late Historical Plays and the Third Reich — 89

5: Schiller from the Left: Early Leftist Criticism and Criticism in the German Democratic Republic — 109

6: The Federal Republic of Germany and Post-(re)unification Criticism — 135

Works Cited — 151

Index — 163

Acknowledgments

MY INDEBTEDNESS TO colleagues and friends cannot be repaid by a mere mention in print, but it would be a sin of omission to refrain from publicly thanking those who have helped me most in my undertaking. Without Professor Jeffrey L. Sammons, this book would never have been written. His graduate seminar on Schiller at Yale University drew my attention to the dramas of the "sentimentalische" poet. His assistance in matters great and small through all stages of the project has been greathearted and invaluable. The patience, insight, and editorial acumen of Professors Steve Dowden and James Hardin have also been crucial. I wish to thank the staff of the library at the University of Oregon, including Bruce Tabb, Henry Wilson, and Aimee Yogi, as well as the entire hard-working Interlibrary Loan Office. The staff at the Schiller-Nationalmuseum and Deutsches Literaturarchiv, in particular Reinhard Tgahrt, also deserve thanks for their helpfulness. Thanks go to colleagues at the University of Oregon, especially Professor Susan Anderson, who have assisted through the rewriting process; I would also like to thank Professors Alex Mathäs and Virpi Zuck, as well as Nigel Cottier. I also want to express my appreciation for the efforts of David Frey, departmental computer technician. Not least of all, I thank friends who have contributed through assorted helpful acts, less academic but no less important, such as child care, cooking, cleaning, and encouragement: Carmel Bender, Tom Dodd, Gay Kramer-Dodd, Kendrick Norris, Andrea Spector, Cynthia Thiessen, and Kermit Westerberg. For the patience of my children, Erik and Maija Anstine, I cannot begin to express my admiration and appreciation.

K. J. S.
February 2001

Introduction

Denn er war unser!
— Johann Wolfgang von Goethe, "Epilog zu Schiller's 'Glocke,'" 1815

Denn er ist unser.
— Johannes R. Becher, "Denn er ist unser: Friedrich Schiller, der Dichter der Freiheit," speech at Becher-Archiv, 1949

Wenn ein Denkmal renoviert wird, kommen unfehlbar die Mauerasseln und Tausendfüßler ans Licht und sagen: Denn er war unser! [When a monument is renovated, the wall lice and centipedes emerge into the light without fail and say: For he was ours!]
— Karl Kraus, "Schrecken der Unsterblichkeit," 1909

THESE PRONOUNCEMENTS ON Friedrich Schiller (1759–1805) — Goethe's reverent words, Becher's politicizing bon mot, Kraus's typically exasperated statement — reflect a process of evaluation and reevaluation, of appropriation and rejection, that continues to this day. Shifts in attitude reflect contemporary aesthetic standards, personal opinion, and political tendentiousness. The present book is a study of such shifts regarding one segment of Schiller's oeuvre, his late historical plays. The movable platform from which such shifts will be observed is itself in flux. From Schiller's time through today, notions about history and about our relationship to it have changed radically and have, of necessity, affected the way in which "historical" portrayal is evaluated. This work will trace these shifts and how they affected criticism of Schiller's late historical plays. As difficult as it is to isolate one aspect of Schiller's work because of the complicated interworkings of his aesthetic, historical, dramaturgical, and philosophical thought, an examination of how his historical plays were viewed in light of the changing conception of history will show why Schiller should be rehabilitated and his plays performed today.

Because of Schiller's prominence and provenance, German critics of all stripes have found themselves moved to come to terms with his production; herein lies one reason for the continual re-evaluation. His plays are the primary subject of this book, but his philosophical and aesthetic writings are every bit as influential as his literary works. Some critics see Schiller as the watershed to modern times as he establishes the prototype of the self-conscious artist in *Über naive und sentimentalische Dichtung* (On Naive and Sentimental Poetry, 1800). His aesthetic project, as outlined primarily in *Die ästhetische Erziehung des Menschen in einer Reihe von Briefen* (The Aesthetic Education of Man in a Series of Letters, 1794), was ambitious and sophisticated: to shape humans through the experience of art to a new stage of awareness. Debate continually returns to the question of whether art should be immanent or functional, and Schiller's letters provide one pole of such debates — the functional one. Schiller's writings on drama, "Über die tragische Kunst" (On Tragedy, 1791–92) and "Über das Pathetische" (On Pathos, 1793) set out a program that determined discussion about the nature of tragedy and theater during most of the nineteenth century and beyond. Indeed, a scholar as closely affiliated with the postmodern as Paul de Man (1919–83) can admit the present age's debt to Schiller: "Perhaps the Schillerian aesthetic categories, whether we know it or not, are still the taken-for-granted premises of our pedagogical, historical, and political ideologies" (266). While a discussion of the extent to which Schiller used his own theories in the dramas he wrote subsequent to the appearance of his philosophical essays lies outside the purview of this study, critics who examined his late plays were certainly aware of Schiller's aesthetic writings and occasionally use these essays to support — and sometimes criticize — Schiller's dramatic work. Like many other writers of his time, Schiller is also indebted to Greek aesthetics; his notions of tragedy can trace their roots to antiquity, and he even reinstates a Greek-style chorus in *Die Braut von Messina* (The Bride of Messina, 1803). Of course, the entire view of art as an instructional tool has much in common with Greek ideas of catharsis, though Schiller's project has the potential for more political applications.

Generally considered more "German" than the cosmopolitan Goethe (1749–1832), Schiller has frequently been called into service for ideological and nationalistic purposes. His engagement with such universal concepts as freedom and education continues to beckon to readers and viewers in successive generations. But Schiller's universal relevance should not lead one to think that his work has been consistently and highly valued throughout the 200 years since its appearance, or that its appeal has always been identified with the same aspects of his production. On the contrary: Schiller has experienced dizzying shifts in popularity that are nearly unequaled in German letters; few writers have been so honored and also so repudiated. For example, during the nineteenth century, anniversary celebrations enjoyed high rates of participation among scholars and "*Volk*" [people] alike; during the Weimar Republic, however, his works were left to collect dust, his idealism perceived as too naive (in the modern sense) for disillusioned Germans after the First World War. His words have been divorced from their context and used for rhetorical effect, and his plays and poems have been well worn in classrooms. Thus, while many speakers of German know who Schiller is, not many know his work in any detail. In particular, not many know how truly radical and experimental his plays were and are.

Criticism of Schiller's late historical plays follows an ebb and flow between concern with the representational and with the universal, a movement coinciding roughly with attitudes toward the representation of history in narrative form. The term *historical drama* has always generated controversy, and the reason becomes more apparent in the German term *historische Dichtung*.[1] Scholars during the Enlightenment pointed out that this term is an oxymoron because, for them, if something was historical, it was not fictitious. The drawing of a distinction between history and fiction goes back at least as far as Aristotle. The literary critic Johann Christoph Gottsched (1700–1766) declared that the poet's task is the representation not of history but of moral truth. Schiller echoes this view in "Über die tragische Kunst" when he distinguishes between historical and poetic truth. But at the same time he recognizes the attraction that historical subjects have for writers of drama, particularly in light of the post-Baroque longing for "nature," for human beings who had actually existed, for a realistic depiction of their lives. Gotthold Ephraim Lessing (1729–81) in his essays on drama, *Hamburgische Dramaturgie* (two volumes, 1767, 1769), gives particular instructions regarding historical drama, while avowing that where a choice is available to a writer between staying true to sources and following artistic considerations, the latter should take precedence. He argues against the use of "historisches Kolorit" — of costumes and other trappings from the time period in question — because such elements alienate the audience and prevent it from being pulled into the magic of the play. But no other term for the genre that uses historical materials in dramatic form has come into general use. In fact, the tension engendered through placing these two seemingly mutually exclusive terms together is stimulating and useful. It falls into place naturally within the discourse of New Historicism, which argues for awareness that historical writing relies on narrative forms that are inherently fictional.

It would be difficult to exaggerate Schiller's contribution to the shaping of the German historical drama. Before Lessing, drama tended to fall into one or more of several categories: it was apolitical; it was borrowed from elsewhere; it provided visual and aural Bible interpretations for the less educated; or it mocked the political, as in the *Haupt- und Staatsaktionen* [roughly translatable as "historical plays"] of the traveling theater companies. To be sure, the great Baroque poet and dramatist Andreas Gryphius (1616–64) made his mark on the stage, but modern German drama had its birth during Schiller's lifetime. He is one of the first secular dramatists to explore the division between history and myth (despite his affinity for Greek aesthetics) and to focus on the individual event rather than, as in Baroque drama, to view what happens on earth not only as *vanitas* but also as unoriginal. To be sure, the prerequisites for the development of German historical drama emerge in the Renaissance and the early Enlightenment. As art and science begin to focus on the empirical, they begin to focus on the individual; in so doing, they become historical. Before Schiller, however, the audience for drama was politically uninterested, not least of all because political power was concentrated in the hands of the few (even during Schiller's time, the middle class had no access to political power). Although Schiller does not write national dramas in the manner of Shakespeare (partly because in German-speaking lands before 1800 there was no central government as there was in Elizabethan England), the influence of Shakespeare is palpable in all the dramatists of the *Sturm und Drang* [Storm and Stress]. His examination of the collisions between the political and personal life is the first on the German stage, with the exception of Goethe's *Egmont* (1788). Schiller's literary descendants — Georg Büchner (1813–37), Christian Dietrich Grabbe (1801–36), and Bertolt Brecht (1898–1956) — display a turn toward a more pessimistic view of politics, but treat similar struggles.

This study will examine a line of criticism of Schiller's later historical dramas — the *Wallenstein* trilogy (1799), *Maria Stuart* (1800), and *Die Jungfrau von Orleans* (The Maid of Orleans, 1801) — a line extending in time from pronouncements by Schiller's contemporaries to Schiller scholarship in the 1990s. Particularly analyzed will be the evaluation of how history was and is perceived (*history* in this sense will include not only the concept of representing the past in narrative form but also historiography itself), along with the effect of this perception on Schiller criticism. The present volume, then, is the result of an attempt to trace a trajectory of fluctuations in historical thought and their contribution to changing attitudes about Schiller's late historical plays — attitudes that belie any notion of "universal appeal."

Although Schiller wrote during an age that tended to view history teleologically, his plays continued to be staged throughout the nineteenth century, an epoch that turned increasingly to a scientific, detail-focused study of history. This view consequently underwent scrutiny after the cataclysmic years surrounding and including the First World War, as well as in the two totalitarian, ideologically focused regimes that marked the mid-century, Adolf Hitler's Third Reich and the German Democratic Republic (GDR). In recent decades historical questions have come center stage again as the postmodern discourse of New Historicism — the disavowal of objectivity and the acknowledgment of how literary forms affect content — has begun to color Schiller criticism.

This study does not claim to be a comprehensive evaluation of either historical theory or Schiller *Rezeptionsgeschichte* [reception history] but a core sampling of important critical texts and their indebtedness to regnant theories of history and historiography. The critical trajectory shows that the popularity of these plays stands in a meaningful relationship to the prevailing attitudes about historical representation and accuracy. The reception of the three plays — Schiller's plays that are most explicitly based on historical sources — will be examined in this context. Although Schiller made deliberate use of historical source material in the creation of these dramas, these sources will not be outlined in any detail, as many studies have already documented them. Finally, though *Die Verschwörung des Fiesko zu Genua* (The Conspiracy of Fiesco in Genoa, 1783) and *Dom Karlos Infant von Spanien* (Don Carlos, Infant of Spain, 1789) are based on historical sources, I have limited this study to completed dramas written after Schiller's professional engagement with historical writing, for they best illustrate the kind of literary criticism I wish to examine.

The historical settings of the plays to be examined are probably familiar to most readers; therefore, only a cursory summary will be provided here. *Wallenstein* is the drama based on material least familiar to an English speaker. The setting for this trilogy, which consists of *Wallensteins Lager* (Wallenstein's Camp), *Die Piccolomini* (The Piccolomini), and *Wallensteins Tod* (Wallenstein's Death), is the Thirty Years' War. The first play, set in the camp of Wallenstein's imperial soldiers, prepares the audience for Wallenstein's appearance in the middle of the second part of the tragedy. Attention in this portion is focused on Octavio Piccolomini, who will take Wallenstein's command after the general is condemned for treason against the emperor, and on Octavio's son, Max, an idealistic imperial officer attached by friendship and soldierly loyalty to Wallenstein. In *Wallensteins Tod* Wallenstein's attempt to negotiate an alliance with Sweden — an alliance compelled by factors that have spiraled out of his control — founders, and he is murdered. The "historical inaccuracies" that are usually mentioned in criticism of this play are the invented figure Max Piccolomini and his love relationship with Thekla, Wallenstein's daughter, as well as the character of Wallenstein, which is repeatedly referred to as more noble and admirable than that of his historical counterpart. Many critics focus, too, on the astrological aspects of the drama, which, while not anachronistic, find a striking prominence in this tragedy.

Maria Stuart presents the last three days of Mary, Queen of Scots; although this play stays closest to its historical sources, there are notable inventions (or, as they are occasionally termed, "*Ausschweifungen*" [aberrations], a word that in German can connote debauchery or excess): Maria and Queen Elizabeth meet face to face in the central scene; both queens are younger than their historical models; an invented character, Mortimer, makes a final attempt to rescue Maria; and Lord Leicester, Elizabeth's historical love interest, is in love with Maria, as well. And *Die Jungfrau von Orleans,* which Schiller subtitled "a romantic tragedy" (a designation that caused, and still causes, considerable controversy and vexation) and which, thus, may be entitled to greater liberties with the historical sources, presents a Joan of Arc who falls in love with an English soldier and dies a national heroine on the battlefield, not a condemned witch at the stake. George Steiner has claimed that if anyone could write a "romantic tragedy," Schiller could — although the term does seem oxymoronic: if a romantic approach intentionally evades the tragic, primarily through transcendence, and if man is perfectible, then there can be no sense of remorse, which is essential to tragedy.

Schiller wrote historiographical essays and served as professor of philosophy at the University of Jena for several years before he returned to writing drama. Even after abandoning his career as a historian he researched his historical dramas thoroughly. A comparison of the line-feet of criticism surrounding Schiller's dramatic and historical works would affirm what critics have been saying for almost two centuries: Schiller was far more successful as a dramatist than as a historian. Although the reception of the historical lectures he delivered at the university (later published in the journal *Merkur*) was initially cordial, by late in the century his historical essays were being openly ridiculed. It is only recently that renewed attention has been paid to these studies for their "radical" combination of literary skill and historical research. Critics often remark on the relationship of Schiller's historical writings to his late historical plays, especially *Wallenstein;* his focus on "historical individuals" rather than events can be seen in both. It is also frequently mentioned, as Otto Johnston reminds us, that history interested Schiller less as a chronicle of what happened than as information about the modern human condition. It is a good idea, as well, to remember that Schiller was more inspired by a philosopher, Immanuel Kant (1724–1804), than by any historian, including August Ludwig von Schlözer (1735–1809). One should also bear in mind that Schiller saw the primary function of theater as education, not entertainment, and that he argued for the theater as a tool for enlightenment, especially in "Die Schaubühne als eine moralische Anstalt betrachtet" (The Stage Seen as a Moral Institution, 1784), as well as in the letters on aesthetic education. Theater "propagated bourgeois virtues and, as political morality, also criticized the dominant social relations" (Berghahn, in Hohendahl, 19). By contrast, his late historical plays have weathered radical shifts in the way history has been understood; indeed, critics have occasionally called them more "historical" than, for example, his essays on the Thirty Years' War and the fall of the Netherlands. It is important to bear in mind that Schiller wrote from a dual mindset that united the study of history in its philosophical sense with an awareness of aesthetics and literary demands. This point is often forgotten by critics who wish to denigrate Schiller's alleged excesses on either side.

Because of Schiller's awareness of historical thought, the first chapter of the present study begins with an examination of the notion of *Universalgeschichte* [universal history], a view of history prevalent at the turn of the eighteenth century; Schiller emphatically embraced this conception. I will present contemporary criticism by Goethe and others in this context. The second chapter turns to Johann Gottfried Herder's (1744–1803) break with universal history and Leopold von Ranke's (1795–1886) "scientific" view. Once the particulars of human experience — historical detail — moved into a more central position, Schiller's plays were either critiqued negatively for their free-handedness in this respect or defended against too scientific a view. At the turn of the next century Ranke's view had lost ground; optimism about the rational, comprehensible world gave way to a darker, more insecure picture. Thus, chapter 3 examines how the writings of Wilhelm Dilthey (1833–1911) and Oswald Spengler (1880–1936), under the influence of Friedrich Nietzsche (1844–1900), affected the way Schiller's plays were viewed.

Chapters 4 and 5 examine what two important ideological stances — Nazism and the Communism of the German Democratic Republic — meant for the interpretation and use of Schiller's late historical plays. While these regimes had clear differences, one can not help but notice the points of contact that their views of Schiller share, particularly in the way his characters are used as anachronistic examples of German patriotism. The final chapter examines the interpretation of Schiller's work in the Federal Republic of Germany (FRG), as well as interpretations by scholars writing in post-reunification Germany after 1989, and moves into the latest phase of Schiller criticism, New Historicist interpretations. Is there a place for Schiller in the postmodern age? In *The Social Responsi-*

bility of the Historian François Bedarida questions the meaningfulness of a historian succumbing to a world without universal values, imploring that "we must choose between scholarship and fiction. What responsibility would remain for the historian if history were merely representation and discourse, as Nietzsche asserted; if there were no truth, but only interpretations?" (5).

While Schiller's intentions — insofar as they may be ascertained — take a back seat in this study, they should not be ignored. In particular, his conception of how art should and can function in society is of vast importance for his work in drama. Schiller articulates his views in the essays mentioned above as well as elsewhere. Seeing in art a vehicle for enlightenment, as Schiller does, creates a schism between artists and those educated by their products. Schiller's attitude toward art was rightly criticized as elitist, and his ideas helped change the nature and purpose of literary criticism: critics became educators as well as arbiters of taste, and the bifurcation of literature into "fine" and "popular" became more pronounced. At the same time, as critics saw that their pedagogical efforts were foundering at the end of the nineteenth century, they became increasingly insular. The function of the critic is today yet again in question, as Jost Hermand and others explore problems inherent in the profession in an effort to find ways out of academic isolation.

In addition, Schiller's letters give insight into his views on history, although it is not easy to find a consistent line of thought in this regard. One of his most famous pronouncements on the difference between history, *Geschichte,* and fiction, *Dichtung,* appears in a letter to Christian Gottfried Körner of January 7, 1788. He says that the philosophical, inner necessity of both forms is the same and that "Wenn eine Geschichte, wäre sie auch auf die glaubwürdigsten Chroniken gegründet, nicht geschehen sein *kann*, d.h. wenn der Verstand den Zusammenhang nicht einsehen kann, so ist sie ein Unding; wenn eine Tragödie nicht geschehen sein *muß*, sobald ihre Voraussetzungen Realität enthalten, so ist sie wieder ein Unding" [When a story, no matter if grounded on the most credible sources, *can* not have happened, that is, when the intellect cannot see the connection, then it is an impossibility; when a tragedy does not *have* to have happened, as soon as its suppositions embody reality, then that, too, is an impossibility] (*Nationalausgabe,*[2] vol. 11, 151). He eventually favors the inner truth of literature over history, because it teaches us "den *Menschen* und nicht *den* Menschen kennen, die Gattung und nicht das sich so leicht verlierende Individuum" [to know *man* and not *that* man, the type and not the individual, so easy to lose track of] (*NA*, vol. 25, 154). As late as 1797 Schiller takes pride in the fact that Aristotle had voiced similar preferences for poetry as more philosophical and ideal than history.

In choosing a method for this study I have taken direction and comfort from Friedrich Schlegel (1772–1829), who claims that if one has a system, one is as lost intellectually as someone who has no system at all — one must sustain both positions (80). I have aimed to incorporate all critics who dealt extensively or interestingly with history or historiography in connection with Schiller's late historical plays. Further, because the field is quite broad, I have focused mainly on German critics. I have also tended to organize the commentary by play and, thereafter, in chronological fashion. Where it makes better sense to speak about all three plays within the discussion of a certain critic for better clarification of his stance, however, I have changed my organizing principles. Anglo-American critics have made increasingly significant contributions to Schiller scholarship in the past forty years, especially as New Historicism begins to exercise influence on German critics. To date, German critics have only set a tentative toe into the treacherous waters of this discourse; books such as *Schiller heute* (Schiller Today) and *Geschichte als Literatur: Formen und Grenzen der Repräsentation von Vergangenheit* (History as Literature: Forms and Limits of the Representation of History), however, show that there has been a relaxing of the suspicion with which Hayden White's theories were first met.

Some challenges arose during the composition of this study. Many critics during the early nineteenth century wrote anonymously; therefore, it is nearly impossible to obtain details about their backgrounds, connections, or gender, although one can assume that most of them were male. It is particularly difficult (and perhaps not even advisable) to retain critical distance while dealing with appropriations of Schiller's plays by Third Reich critics. There is also the problem of changing connotations of vocabulary. I have used the word *history* to denote the broader notion of recorded past experience — a notion that changes through time — and *historiography* for the actual narrative that is recorded as a representation of history. The meaning of the German term *Historismus*, translated as "historicism," is one that scholars continue to debate, although most agree that it deals with the notion of one's own time and place defining one's perspective. In the main, it refers to the placing of information into its own historical context, while bearing in mind the historical context of the placer.

I profess my admiration for New Historicist approaches to literary study. One tenet of this approach is the belief that the reporting of history is an activity dependent on literary forms. It is, perhaps, a foolhardy project to attempt a historical study in postmodern times. I hope, nevertheless, to shed some light on how the esteem in which Schiller's late historical plays are held — an esteem I share — remains dependent on the historical context in which they were analyzed. I predict a Schiller renaissance in the decades to come, not only because the historical ebb and flow of his popularity indicates such a development but also because of his significance in postmodern times. One aim of this book is to show why, in struggling with the representation of the truth and with the moral issues that obtain, Schiller must find relevance in times when the trajectory of many postmodern approaches finds an endpoint in anarchy and annihilation.

Except where noted, all translations are mine. In accordance with the guidelines of the *Literary Criticism in Perspective* series, a list of works cited, arranged in alphabetical order, appears at the end of this introduction and of each chapter, and an overall list, organized in chronological order, appears at the end of the volume.

Notes

[1] *Dichtung* is a translator's nightmare. English equivalents range from "literature" to "fiction" to "poetry"; one connotation is "fabulating."

[2] Hereafter, the *Nationalausgabe*, the National Edition of Schiller's works, will be referred to as "*NA*."

Works Cited

Bedarida, François, ed. *The Social Responsibility of the Historian*. Providence RI and Oxford: Berghahn, 1994.

de Man, Paul. *The Rhetoric of Romanticism*. New York: Columbia UP, 1984.

Goethe, Johann Wolfgang von. *Werke*, ed. Erich Trunz, vol. 1. Munich: Beck, 1981.

Hinck, Walter, ed. *Geschichte als Schauspiel. Deutsche Geschichtsdramen: Interpretationen*. Frankfurt am Main: Suhrkamp, 1981.

Hohendahl, Peter Uwe, ed. *A History of German Literary Criticism, 1730–1980*. Lincoln and London: U of Nebraska P, 1988.

Johnston, Otto. "Schillers politische Welt," in *Schiller-Handbuch*, ed. Helmut Koopmann. Stuttgart: Körner, 1998, 44–69.

Kollektiv für Literaturgeschichte. *Johannes R. Becher*, ed. Horst Gorsch. Berlin: Volk und Wissen, 1967.

Kraus, Karl. "Schrecken der Unsterblichkeit," in his *Werke*, ed. Heinrich Fischer, vol. 12. Munich and Vienna: Langen, 1964, 233–37.

Schlegel, Friedrich von. *Kritische Ausgabe seiner Werke*, ed. Ernst Behler, vol. 18. Munich and Zurich: Schoningh, 1979.

Sengle, Friedrich. *Das historische Drama in Deutschland: Geschichte eines literarischen Mythos*. Stuttgart: Metzler, 1969.

Steiner, George. *The Death of Tragedy*. New York: Knopf, 1961.

1: The Legacy of the Enlightenment: Criticism by Schiller's Contemporaries

THE GERMAN ENLIGHTENMENT was not a period of unified attitudes toward the nature and progress of history, and for this reason it is problematic to speak of "Enlightenment theories of history." As a starting point, however, one can use the model that dominated Enlightenment thinking, that of *Universalgeschichte*. This theory posits mankind's (in this chapter I intentionally use noninclusive language to underscore the masculine focus of the period) progression through history toward a higher moral state, a movement perceived as analogous to the development of the individual human being. During the Enlightenment a shift occurred from the long-standing assumption that a divine power held sway at the center of this system to the possibility that man himself held the reins of his historical destiny. Naturally, not all thinkers subscribed to the removal of God from the center of the system. This new view, though secular, was, nevertheless, teleological, positing mankind as perfected by the end of its trajectory. Common to all notions under the rubric *Universalgeschichte* is the idea of a meaningful, centralized relationship between all events and experiences of the human condition.

By the end of the seventeenth century the plausibility of universal history was questioned by some, a reevaluation that bears certain similarities to recent New Historicist debate. Great advances in the natural sciences during the century had led to the attempt to apply scientific methods of examination to subjects such as philosophy and history. But the movement toward freer intellectual inquiry was still restrained by the influence of the Church. Peter Hanns Reill describes the result of the intellectual struggles of this period as "an unstable mixture of classical, medieval, and humanist elements circumscribed by and crammed into the traditional Christian interpretation of universal history" (9).

Eventually, historiography settled into a bifurcated form; on one side lay the study of the broad sweep of historical movement, on the other the examination of particular historical details. Between these two currents there existed no connecting relationship. The gap was recognized, and attempts were made to reconcile the two approaches; the difficulties proved to be insurmountable. Instead, Enlightenment thinkers seemed obliged either to focus on a smoothly flowing process of history or to advocate sharpening methods of documenting historical particulars. The eminent historian August Ludwig von Schlözer came closest to uniting the two lines; he critiqued the traditional listing of kings, battles, and alliances and developed in his *Vorstellung seiner Universal-Historie* (Interpretation of His Universal History, 1772) the secular version of *Universalgeschichte,* which was to become popular in German-speaking lands during Schiller's time. His method incorporated both sides of the dichotomy, while, at the same time, positing a traditional telos for mankind's moral progress. Schlözer was, however, unable to put his ideas into practice. As the Enlightenment came to a close, the idea of the "broad sweep," a view entirely commensurate with *Universalgeschichte,* emerged the winner.

Although the challenges to *Universalgeschichte* were mounted well before the end of the eighteenth century, most German fin-de-siècle thinkers still subscribed to some version of it. Certainly the prominent thinkers who wrestled with notions of history in essays that reflect the importance of these issues at the time — Kant in his *Idee zu einer allgemeinen Geschichte im weltbürgerlichen Absicht* (Idea of a Universal History from a Cosmopolitan Point of View, 1784), Friedrich Wilhelm Joseph von Schelling (1775–1854) in his *System des transcendentalen Idealismus* (System of Transcendental Idealism, 1800), and Johann Gottlieb Fichte (1762–1814) in his *Grundzüge des gegenwärtigen Zeitalters* (Characteristics of the Present Age, 1804–1805) — describe systems that correspond to this heading. Schiller falls into line with these compatriots, seeing history as the continuing struggle toward ideal freedom.

During the Enlightenment critics had begun to wield political power — not as politicians or rulers per se, but in a broader sense as educators. Their function was not only to raise up objects of art worthy for the perusal of a growing, increasingly literate bourgeoisie but also to shape opinion and an accompanying political consciousness. As journals increase in number and gain in importance and readership, the examination of the attitudes toward history becomes not merely interesting but crucial. Schiller himself, as one would guess, believed firmly in this pedagogical function of the critic. In fact, that function was the overt purpose of *Die Horen,* the journal that he and Goethe launched. This publication was intended to present the finest works of art for the purpose of edifying its readership. But the level and tone of the journal were lofty; *Die Horen* was heavily criticized for what were perceived as elitist tendencies. Schiller countered by reiterating the role of the critic in helping those incapable of understanding such art to rise to a level of enlightenment that would render them able to appreciate high aesthetic achievement.

But Romantic critics such as the Schlegels, who believed that art should be separated from any notions of functionality, criticized Schiller's lack of concern for *Volkstümlichkeit* [a difficult term to translate; "popularity" comes close, but the German word has nationalistic overtones]. In other words, during a time when nationalism was beginning to make headway, Schiller was accused of turning his back on the people in condescension and elitism. He rejected this charge, for he saw *Volkstümlichkeit* as a misguided attempt to reinstate a Homeric unity, a project that in his eyes was doomed to failure. The Schiller of *Die Räuber* (The Robbers, 1781) — the quintessential *Sturm und Drang* play — was now seen as a reactionary by the Romantic camp.

Several stances regarding the function of the literary critic were thus in play during the last years of Schiller's life. With these lines drawn, we can turn to the criticism of Schiller's plays itself to determine how *Universalgeschichte* may or may not have colored it.

Wallenstein

For various reasons, the *Wallenstein* trilogy drew more critical attention in the years immediately following its appearance (as well as in the centuries thereafter) than the other two plays considered here, *Maria Stuart* and *Die Jungfrau von Orleans.* Its sheer length — a prologue and a brief "comedy" followed by two five-act tragedies — provides one explanation. Second, *Wallensteins Lager* was Schiller's first play after a twelve-year hiatus; its appearance would have been eagerly anticipated for this reason alone. Another plausible explanation is that in a period where nationalistic feelings were first awakening, it is the only play of the three set in

German-speaking lands. Because the trilogy draws on a prior work by Schiller, *Geschichte des Dreißigjährigen Kriegs* (History of the Thirty Years' War, 1791–93), it demanded certain comparisons. And, finally, it may be said that the work provided a radical break from the theater productions of the day in terms of subject matter and language. *Wallensteins Lager* presented members of the lower classes in a different, more serious light; previously, they had only been portrayed in comedies (some critics classify this part of the trilogy a comedy for that reason). The music, the costumes, and the *Knittelvers* (doggerel) of *Wallensteins Lager* were commented on by nearly every contemporary reviewer.

It has been established that the conversations between Schiller and Goethe about the writing of *Wallenstein* and about the concurrent staging of Goethe's *Egmont* must have influenced the development of the trilogy. Goethe's *Götz von Berlichingen* (1787) has been identified as the first true German historical play, and for a time he, too, was intensely occupied with questions surrounding the representation of history. He was initially eager to find a way to make drama more historical and national, and *Egmont* was his crowning effort. Unlike Schiller, however, Goethe appropriates material from a time not far from the present and attempts to enlighten both past and present at once.

At the play's debut it was noted that Goethe "got away" with having the characters appear in costumes of the time depicted, a move that went against Lessing's dictum that dramatists should not make the scenery and the other trappings of the theater conform to the time being portrayed because doing so would be too alienating for the audience. The acceptance of this shift by Goethe bore witness to the success of an entirely new form of historical drama. Perhaps what is most striking is the individual depiction of the main character as an individual rather than as a cardboard representation of a historical figure known to all from schoolbooks. Critics also chided Goethe for playing with the facts, for up until this time historical drama was supposed to stick to them (Sengle, 38). He had the potential to be a major influence on the development of this genre; ultimately, however, he found history to be just one fruitful source among many for dramatic material. *Egmont,* Goethe's farewell to historical drama, was not as enthusiastically received as *Wallenstein;* was it because his interests had already drifted elsewhere? Friedrich Sengle sees the difference in reception as stemming from the dramatists' lives: while Goethe could assume freedom as a given, Schiller could not. Schiller's historical dramas reflect a lifelong struggle for freedom to an entire class involved in the same project on a larger scale. Sengle goes so far as to attribute the creation of Schiller's new, politically idealistic historical dramas — ones that expanded the consciousness of the eighteenth-century German bourgeoisie — to the difficult years he spent in the Karlsschule.

In a letter to Heinrich Meyer (January 1, 1797) and in his critical essays on the *Wallenstein* trilogy Goethe assumes Lessing's point of view regarding the poetic privilege of the writer in dealing with historical materials. Lessing advocated complete freedom to change such materials for poetic purposes, because the poet's purpose in writing a drama is not to write historiography (*Hamburgische Dramaturgie*, Stück 23, 24). Goethe claims that the differences between the historical Albrecht von Wallenstein (1583–1634) and Schiller's creation, which he enumerates, are important for the simple reason that Schiller had to have had a reason to make such changes. In a review published a few months later, on the occasion of the debut of the second part of *Wallenstein,* he notes that the actions of Schiller's Wallenstein become more difficult to understand and, thus, he becomes more suspicious, while the historical Wallenstein had a deep-rooted belief in astrology that made him more likely to mull over the past, present, and future than to decide and act quickly. He claims as the main point of the play the representation of a remarkable existence that goes awry because of unfortunate timing as well as its conflict with life's vulgar reality and with the integrity of human nature. Goethe thus sees Schiller's task as the portrayal of two contradictory objects: Wallenstein's spirit, which is characterized by greatness and idealism as well as by near-insanity and criminality, and "life's vulgar reality," which touches the moral and rational as well as the small, petty, and contemptible. In the middle, claims Goethe, stands love. In this analysis one can detect Goethe's justification for the addition of the fictitious story of Max and Thekla's relationship (few of Schiller's other contemporaries refer to the fact that Schiller invented the figure of Max).

Conscious as he was of Schiller's view of the theater as a "moralische Anstalt," Goethe is clearly interested in the effect Schiller's trilogy has on its audience. In the first place, plays are most obviously an opportunity to learn about history in a more than merely passive way because of the nature of the theatrical experience. In the case of *Wallenstein,* Goethe proposes that viewers engage in active discussion of what they remember about the history of the Thirty Years' War, either with other members of the audience or within their own minds. In so doing, they begin to differentiate between the poetical and the historical and to see the difference between the playwright as historian and as creator. One connection the thoughtful theater-goer may make is the hidden story of the Girondist general Charles Dumouriez (1739–1823), who after his embarrassing defeat went over to the Austrian side to avoid dismissal and was convicted of treason. Goethe also mentions how the *Knittelvers* used in *Wallensteins Lager* conveys the viewer back to the Thirty Years' War; here is a point of departure from Lessing's anti-*Kolorit* edict.

Goethe also discusses the goblet in the banquet scene; episodes from Bohemia's history are depicted on this vessel, and the cellarmaster describes them. This scene, according to Goethe, gives Schiller a convenient opportunity to provide historical information about Bohemia and, thus, about Wallenstein's interest in the country. Goethe also brings to the reader's attention the fact that the setting of the play itself, the beginning of the Thirty Years' War, is represented on the goblet. We will have reason to return to this intriguing vessel.

Goethe is a clear admirer of Schiller's historical trilogy, and he pronounced it an exceptional achievement. He supported Schiller's right to mold the historical material to suit his artistic purposes, and he saluted the educational aspects, as well. On the whole, however, one feels that Goethe has moved beyond historical concerns — most of his reviews do not deal with historical aspects at all.

Another interpreter who notes the ability of the *Wallenstein* trilogy to transport the audience into a certain historical realm is the prominent Weimar critic Karl August Böttiger, writing for the *Journal des Luxus und der Moden* (1798). He mentions the accuracy of the costumes and the appropriateness of the *Knittelvers* to the time in question. He also raises racial-national issues in *Die Piccolomini* as he sees in certain characters representatives of their respective cultures: Octavio Piccolomini has "die ränkevollste Kälte des Italiäners" [the most cunning coldness of the Italian]; the Swedish Carl Gustaf Wrangel (1613–76), on the other hand, displays reserve, stubborn conviction, and his rhetoric is the "bibelveste Kernsprache des Schweden" [Bible-firm pithy speech of the Swede] (quoted in Fambach, 434). In such commentary one finds aspects of racial categorization that bring Herder to mind. In 1799 Böttiger published another review that refers to the historical material itself: he says that Schiller wrestles with it but does not do it "violence." One wonders precisely where the line between acceptable and unacceptable variation might be, but Böttiger does not elaborate.

Yet another critic, this one anonymous, argues against requiring historical accuracy of Schiller. In a thirteen-page review in the *Jahrbücher der preußischen Monarchie* (January-April 1799) this critic evaluates *Die Piccolomini* after its Berlin debut. The reviewer agrees with Lessing in defending Schiller's manipulation of historical "fact," adding, however, that it is an advantage when fact and poetic representation coincide. The critic is especially pleased that the dramatic Wallenstein's character is, as he sees it, exactly the way it was in history. The reviewer does use the term *Abschweifungen* [diversions] to describe the "liberties" taken with the historical facts; this word is reminiscent of the derogatory *Ausschweifungen*, mentioned in the introduction. The historically charged goblet receives mention, but in a more deprecating fashion than Goethe describes it. This writer's complaint is that the long-winded excursus inspired by the goblet is itself unhistorical and unrealistic; a cellar-master would not be likely to have the time to give such full historical commentary, never mind being able to convey it with such fluency. At the same time, the speech is deemed justifiable, if awkward, for the purposes of transmitting historical background. The danger, according to the reviewer, is that those with little familiarity with Wallenstein's history will be confused and distracted from the more important story line.

Another reviewer who analyzed *Wallenstein* before it was released in printed form was W. Süvern, who wrote an influential study examining the debt of the play to Greek tragedy. Before turning to the play itself, he admonishes his readers about the nature of art and criticism: all works of art proceed from a single impulse, and it is the critic's duty to identify this impulse; the audience must attempt to raise itself to the level of the work of art. Here he sounds distinctly like Schiller himself; in his final assessment, however, Süvern avers that *Wallenstein* did not succeed in leaving the audience with a harmonious feeling but, rather, with the specter of gruesome destruction (Hegel will raise similar objections).

The appearance of the printed version of the *Wallenstein* trilogy generated a fresh series of reviews. An anonymous piece in the *Göttingische Anzeigen von gelehrten Sachen* (August 11, 1800) notes the realistic costumes and scenery. (It seems that Lessing's prohibition of such things is rather universally dismissed by now.) The reviewer complains that too much time is spent on "ausführlichen Darstellung gemeiner Gegenstände" [portraying members of the lower class of soldiers in detail]. The review goes on to criticize the character of the historical Wallenstein; oddly, the problem cited is Schiller's alleged *excessive* historical accuracy. The author, according to the reviewer, should be more concerned with maintaining poetic rather than historical integrity. He does not need to worry about how the main character acted in real life, exactly how the actual events unfolded, or whether the characters resemble the individuals depicted. More important is that the audience easily grasp and understand the character; it cannot do so if the character harbors internal contradictions, even though such is often the case with historical personages (Braun SG, 389).[1] On the other hand, a review in the *Neue Würzburger gelehrte Anzeigen* in 1801 points to Schiller's mastery of the chaotic confusion of events, personalities, and intrigues surrounding Wallenstein, praising the poetic genius who is able to tame the unruly historical materials. The product of this taming is a more palatable version of history for the audience. Pedagogical concerns are, thus, mentioned in at least two reviews during this time.

An anonymous reviewer in Leipzig in the same year asks a series of questions related to how the historical material is treated in the poetic product, concluding that the more the poet can display knowledge of the events from which the material is chosen, the more suspect a critic is if he attacks changes that the poet has made to the material (Braun S, 10). This comment traces a connection between a writer's research abilities and poetic abilities that might be difficult to support in some cases. The reviewer lists a few of the differences between the historical facts and Schiller's drama, for example, that Count Matthias von Gallas (1584–1647), not Octavio Piccolomini, took over Wallenstein's command. The reviewer's conclusion is that one can claim not that this Wallenstein is unhistorical but, rather, that he is only partially historical. The tragic element of this play, says the critic, is that what brought about Wallenstein's fall is never directly represented onstage; therefore, we see that he is a victim of his own greatness and ambition. The reviewer finds the use of astrology effective not only because it is historically appropriate but also because it provides a convincing explanation for Wallenstein's attachment to Octavio, the man who is plotting his downfall.

Although the title of his article could intimate a pedagogical purpose for criticism, the prominent Berlin critic Garlieb Merkel tends to favor aesthetic immanence over the functionality of art. Merkel, a Livonian active in Berlin literary circles and a friend of Herder's, protests Schiller's overly accurate handling of the historical material in published letters to an unnamed young woman, "Briefe an ein Frauenzimmer über die wichtigsten Produkte der schönen Literatur" (Letters to a Lady on the Most Important Products of Belles Lettres, 1801). He reports that the initial reaction of the audience on seeing Wallenstein consulting his astrologer was disapproval and disappointment; in Merkel's opinion, Schiller should not have shown weakness in his hero. He mentions the possibility of seeing the play as a poetic-historical portrait, quoting directly from Lessing by name to support what Schiller has done: "der wahre Dichter, sagt Lessing irgendwo, wird nicht das Drama um des historischen Faktums willen schreiben, sondern dieses wählen, weil es sich zu jenem eignet, und wo das nicht ist, hat er freie Macht, durch Aenderungen nachzuhelfen" [The true poet, Lessing says somewhere, will not write a drama for the sake of the historical facts, but rather choose these while they are suited to the former, and where this is not so, he has the freedom to help (the material) by means of alterations] (Braun S, 27). In this way Schiller could have left out the weakness of his hero and still remained true to history. As he stands, Wallenstein is not a good tragic figure, because his indecisiveness bears witness to weakness of character. Schiller is deemed too realistic, because this excessive reliance on historical detail cripples his aesthetic project. Merkel would prefer to see Schiller adhere to more standard principles of tragedy by presenting a protagonist with one only flaw instead of an inherently weak hero. While in this review Merkel criticizes *Wallenstein* for several other reasons, including his opinion that the plot is actually a series of three separate ones, his view of Schiller's work became more positive thereafter, and he was responsible for the playwright's increasing popularity in Berlin circles.

Another critic, writing in the *Allgemeine Literatur-Zeitung* in 1801, sets up a nature-history dichotomy. This critic claims that Schiller wished not to sweep away the inconsistencies of the historical Wallenstein — something that a French poet would do – but, rather, to find a focal point within the inconsistencies. The critic refers to the Prologue in support of this notion, quoting the exact expression: "jedes *äußerste in dem schwankenden Charakter,* wie es im Prolog heißt, zur Natur zurückführen" [to bring each *extremity of the vacillating character,* as it is described in the Prologue, back to Nature] (Braun S, 39). The reviewer compliments Schiller on showing Wallenstein's greatness through the supporting characters, claiming that this technique is essential in highlighting a historical figure. When the hero speaks for himself, however, his weaknesses become apparent, and this exposure of his vulnerability is not dramatically motivated. The reviewer says that the play would have been more successful had Schiller followed history more closely — not for the sake of accuracy but because, the reviewer is convinced, the historical Wallenstein was a less vacillating character than Schiller's poetic one. A direct mention of the issue of historical accuracy occurs when the reviewer speaks of the liberties (albeit permissible ones) Schiller takes with the material; the way the poet uses them, argues the reviewer, provides an excellent example for other writers wishing to use historical sources. He uses the examples of Illo and Buttler to make his case. In reality, Illo was the officer denied advancement because of Wallenstein's intervention; Schiller transfers this situation to Buttler in order to better motivate his complicity in Wallenstein's assassination. The events are thus "true," but the characters are switched. Only in this sense of the word *misrepresentation,* according to this reviewer, has Schiller violated the historical materials.

The critics Fessler and Rhode, writing in *Eunomia* in Berlin in January 1801, return to the golden goblet but in a less deprecatory fashion than the earlier reviewer. Instead of seeing a senseless and dulling excursus into the uninteresting past, these critics deem the goblet "eine bequeme Veranlassung ... mehrere historische und statistische Notizen über das damahlige Böhmen beizubringen" [a convenient reason ... to impart various historical and statistical notes on contemporary Bohemia] (Braun S, 75) — these words are almost a direct quotation from Goethe's review, although he is given no credit for them. Wallenstein's character, however, does not fare as well with Fessler and Rhode. They claim that the viewer comes the theater aware of Wallenstein's greatness but is met with a weak character. Because of this subversion of expectations, the audience is disturbed; the author should have united the dramatic character with the historical one in a smoother, less jarring fashion.

Invented characters are mentioned here for the first time since Goethe's initial review; they receive little praise. They are criticized, however, not for their fictitiousness but for their flawed natures. Thekla is too unfeminine; Gräfin Terzky is unconvincing, and her suicide is dramaturgically unprepared. Schiller is also censured for seldom uniting the ideal and the real, poetry and history. As an example of this fault the reviewers refer to the fact that the goblet is examined in the foreground, while the real action — one of the key scenes of the play — is taking place behind it and must wait "bis der gelehrte, schwatzhafte Kellermeister mit seiner Becherexegese fertig ist" [until the erudite, chatty Master of the Cellar is finished with his goblet exegesis] (Braun S, 75). In other words, the cellarmaster is an inappropriate history teacher who chooses an inappropriate time and place to teach a class.

An anonymous review in the *Neue allgemeine deutsche Bibliothek*, published in Berlin and Stettin in 1801, focuses on the genre of the "historisches Schauspiel" [historical drama] and compares the play, not unfavorably, to Shakespeare's *Henry IV*. Like the other reviewers, this one finds *Wallensteins Lager*, in particular, realistic and capable of transporting the viewer into the times portrayed; the concluding song, the "Reuterlied," is important in this connection because it "giebt unserer Phantasie einen Schwung, der uns die Vergangenheit in eine höchst täuschende Gegenwart verwandelt" [gives our imagination a momentum that transforms the past into a highly deceptive present] (Braun S, 125). Once again, the dramatist is applauded for not following the historical Wallenstein too closely but improving on him by making him more attractive to the viewer. Schiller is commended for uniting the historical and dramatic elements, and this union makes the viewers' hearts sympathetic to Wallenstein.

To summarize, the *Wallenstein* criticism that refers to the portrayal of history or historical elements can be separated roughly into two areas: first, complaints about the presentation of vulgar, unworthy subjects on stage — that is, "too much realism," including commentary on what kind of Wallenstein fulfills the re-

r a tragic hero; and second, comments on Schiller's
historical facts, most of which indicate that the re-
[...]es of how Schiller has done so. There seems to be no
[d]isapproval of lack of accuracy per se.

[...tr]ibutes were written following Schiller's unexpected
[death in] 1805, and some of them looked back at the three
plays under examination here. An anonymous eulogy in the *Allgemeine Literatur-Zeitung* speaks of his use of historical material. Critics once again call Lessing's *Hamburgische Dramaturgie* into service to support Schiller's alteration of the facts (relying on the same quote that Merkel used when speaking about *Wallenstein*) — for example, of Buttler instead of the historical Leslie hiring the assassins in *Wallenstein*. The reviewer wished to prove that Schiller was not attempting to re-create the historical scene but had other things in mind: namely, Wallenstein's spiritual individuality. Schiller's goal was, thus, not historical accuracy but the representation of history as a tragic world.

It is speculative to assume that these critics were aware of *Universalgeschichte* and that a lack of insistence on historical accuracy reveals adherence to the prevalent Enlightenment attitude to history. It is evident, as well, that historical drama is a new concept to the critics who mention it, for, outside of Shakespeare, they mention no predecessors, not even *Götz von Berlichingen* or *Egmont*. It seems that critics are beginning to become conscious of the potentially fertile relationship between drama and history. This consciousness is also arising within writers themselves, for the century produced German literature's finest examples of historical drama in writers such as Christian Dietrich Grabbe and Franz Grillparzer (1791–1872).

We now turn to the other two plays. Although other issues are at stake, the critical literature devoted to *Maria Stuart* and *Die Jungfrau von Orleans*, though sparser than the commentary generated by *Wallenstein*, follows the lines drawn thus far.

Maria Stuart

Of the three plays discussed in this study, *Maria Stuart* is accorded the least commentary; indeed, it has provoked the least controversy throughout the past 200 years. This tragedy, which relies more heavily on historical sources than any other play by Schiller, reminded many reviewers of Shakespeare — to some extent, no doubt, because it is set in Shakespeare's Elizabethan England, but also because Schiller was obviously influenced by Shakespeare's adaptations of historical materials in his dramas. It is, above all, the fictitious meeting of the two queens, Elizabeth I (1533–1603), and Mary Stuart, Queen of Scots (1542–87), that elicits the most negative criticism. In an anonymous review in the *Journal des Luxus und der Moden* from Weimar (July 1800) this meeting is, nevertheless, rationalized on the basis of dramaturgical considerations. The critic praises Schiller's bravery in sacrificing historical reality to the "höhern Forderungen der dramatischen Kunst" [higher demands of dramatic art] (Braun SG, 384), particularly to bring the undramatically indecisive historical Elizabeth to a dramatic, quick decision. The reviewer goes so far as to say that had a meeting occurred, it would certainly have taken the form Schiller dictated.

Fessler and Rhode, in *Eunomia* (April 1801), are as critical of this play as they were of *Die Piccolomini*. They see a grand destiny trivialized in the "kleinliche Leidenschaft eines elenden Weibes" [petty passion of a miserable woman] (Braun S, 84) presented in the name of history. In like manner, they castigate Schiller for bringing the tawdry elements of Maria's past into the work, believing that doing so makes her a less worthy subject for a tragedy. Thus, Schiller is criticized once again for excessive historical accuracy. (In an ironic twist, however, they say that Schiller's ability to create such a work of beauty out of such unworthy material bears witness to his genius.) Two examples of inaccuracies are mentioned: the meeting of the queens and Leicester's love for Maria. But, the reviewers maintain, the poet is, in general, not required to hold himself so slavishly to the historical materials that the literary work becomes flawed. It is the historical truth that should be sacrificed, not the drama. Lessing's precepts hold sway here as they did the discussion of *Wallenstein*.

In June 1801 a review appeared in the *Göttingische Anzeigen von gelehrten Sachen* that is far more positive than Fessler and Rhode's. Immediately, two of Schiller's inventions are revealed — the fictitious character Mortimer and the love relationship between Maria and Leicester — but they are not criticized for being unhistorical. The reviewer goes on, instead, to discuss the character of Elizabeth, which, because it has been modeled closely on historical sources, is lacking in charm. Soon the meeting of the queens is mentioned, and while its lack of historicity is remarked on, the reviewer says that this meeting is part of the beauty of the play. The inventions are, thus, perceived as positive additions to the aesthetic success of the drama. Later in 1801 a brief review in the *Gothaische gelehrte Zeitungen* quotes the Scottish Enlightenment historian William Robertson (1721–93) to support Schiller's characterizations, showing how Maria's guard Paulet, for example, though "rough and harsh, was nevertheless a man of integrity and honour" (Braun S, 102). For the reviewer this play, because it stands in harmony with its sources, provides a model for other historical fiction.

Merkel makes the same complaint as Fessler and Rhode regarding Schiller's apparent need to expose all facts, no matter how disagreeable, when he writes to his young friend about *Maria Stuart* in 1801. He claims that what the audience looks for on stage is not proof that the author has read the historical sources but a work of art from which anything that can cause damage to its artistic value has been removed. In line with his prioritizing of the poetic over the historical, Merkel is annoyed by the confrontation between Burleigh and Maria. In this scene Burleigh attempts to inform Maria that she has been sentenced to death; Maria raises justifiable objections to nearly every point he makes. Nevertheless, Merkel calls the fourteen-page text a tiresome squabbling discussion of the justness or injustice of the judges' behavior. Like Fessler and Rhode, Merkel objects to the use of the stage as a pedagogical forum — at least when the teaching is done directly. The value of art over transmission of historiographical information is clear. Merkel has clearly Romantic tendencies in desiring to keep the art object autonomous.

In 1802 an unsigned review in the *Allgemeine Literatur-Zeitung* also mentions Robertson and his judgment of Mary Stuart. What is to be found in this source, the reviewer maintains, makes Mary an unlikely subject for a representation of pathos; here we assume that the reviewer is referring to Schiller's essay, "Über das Pathetische" (1801) — in other words, is using Schiller's own tools to attack him. This reviewer returns continually to the historical materials, pointing out what Schiller should have used (Mary's perception of her execution as martyrdom for the faith, for example) in order to follow more closely his own criteria for a worthy tragic subject. He points out historical inaccuracies but does not criticize them; in fact, he commends the play for providing a more plausible psychological analysis of Elizabeth than what is found in historical sources, expressing surprise that the queen of England could have laughed and joked as she signed the warrant for execution. The sources explain something that Schiller leaves unexplored in his drama: Burleigh's suspiciously zealous insistence on Maria's execution. According to the reviewer, historical sources reveal that Burleigh feared imprisonment and execution himself were Maria to ascend the throne. Finally, the reviewer approaches an issue that has engaged historians and other scholars throughout the centuries and most recently has concerned New Historicists: on which aspect of Elisabeth's character should the poet focus? Which series of events should one select in the representation of the past, and how should one fill in the gaps that necessarily obtain? The main points of the plot are given; it seems, according to this reviewer, that the poet is as justified in filling the gaps between them as is the historian. The criticism of *Maria Stuart* reveals concerns similar to those raised in the discussion of *Wallenstein* — above all, that dramatic works should look more to poetic achievement than to historical accuracy or pedagogy, regardless of the subject matter. Historical accuracy is still mentioned, though without value being placed on it.

Die Jungfrau von Orleans

Whereas the *Wallenstein* trilogy was met with almost universal enthusiasm, Schiller's dramatization of the historical materials regarding Joan of Arc (1412–31) perplexed public and critics alike. The trouble originates in the historical material itself, which included supernatural wonders and voices as part of the written record. This mixture of the real and the mystical was problematic for Enlightenment historians: they viewed the Middle Ages as an inferior period, in part, because it was perceived as an era of rampant superstition and lack of reason. Schiller was among the first to write about the "Dark Ages," completing his essay "Über Völkerwanderung, Kreuzzüge und Mittelalter" (About Mass Migration, Crusades and the Middle Ages) in 1792. The drama's subtitle, *romantische Tragödie,* was a conundrum for his contemporaries and, indeed, for later scholars; one common interpretation is that *romantic* is used to refer to the Middle Ages. Another issue that made the play problematic — although such unease is not expressed explicitly in the reviews — was the growing threat of French domination in German-speaking areas during the early years of the nineteenth century.

Ernst Brandes belonged to a group of critics and other intellectuals who continued to adhere to an Enlightenment mindset and much preferred Schiller's *Don Carlos* to anything else he ever wrote. This group tended to find Schiller's later plays too saturated with philosophy, affected, and lacking in simplicity and clarity. Of course, one wonders how critics searching for simplicity could praise the mind-boggling plot contortions of the earlier play or how they reconciled Schiller's competing poetic impulses (Schiller himself called the play a failure). Brandes was a major reviewer for the *Göttingische Anzeigen von gelehrten Sachen* from 1801 to 1810; he published his review of *Die Jungfrau von Orleans* shortly after its premiere in 1801. He mentions how Joan's predictions of certain historical events (the discovery of America, for example) and her fight with the Dark Knight disqualify the play as a *historical* tragedy and earn it the adjective *romantic* instead. Brandes refers to Schiller's mastery at representing historical events in his *Geschichte des Abfalles der Niederlande* (History of the Defeat of the Netherlands, 1788); in *Die Jungfrau von Orleans* this skill is missing. By Brandes's account, the protagonist is unbelievable even when viewers use their imagination.

Reviewing the play in the *Allgemeine Literatur-Zeitung* (January 1802), Johann Apel points out that merely by using Joan's name Schiller has created a historical play and has thus obliged himself to follow the historical materials. The writer who chooses to dramatize a historical figure, he says, has the task of setting the poetical character on the stage while causing the audience to summon forth the knowledge it has of the person. In this way the writer's duty becomes that of uniting the poetic and the historical. Schiller accomplishes this unification in his Prologue when Bertrand reports on the state of events in France (the English victories, the impending treason of the Burgundians) and Johanna (Joan) is moved to become France's savior. Apel however, thinks that Schiller sins against the expectations of the genre when Johanna performs unnatural feats and makes prophecies that unwaveringly prove to be accurate. It is clear that by 1802 historical drama has become a firm genre, at least partially because of the popularity of *Wallenstein* and *Maria Stuart*.

Merkel's comments to his friend on *Die Jungfrau von Orleans* are every bit as skeptical as those of other reviewers. He emphasizes the "romantic" aspect of the play, by which he means that the reality portrayed conceals everything that does not engage the imagination and emotions. He turns next to the historical background and then focuses on the play itself. It is, he states, a historical character portrait in Shakespearean style, and its main character, Johanna, stands at the juncture between the historical and the fantastic. This feature causes Merkel difficulties, particularly in the case of the Dark Knight; through the appearance of this fantastic character, the historical play becomes a fairy tale [*Mährchen*], and the illusion is destroyed. As long as we cannot see "das Wunderbare" [the miraculous] in Johanna, we can suspend our disbelief and view this play as a romantic historical drama; once we are confronted by a supernatural being on the stage, a reasonable limitation has been exceeded. Merkel expresses this problem as one that has proved difficult not only for Schiller but also for previous writers who have used the material. For although the miraculous elements in the historical sources beckon writers to treat this material, it is precisely those elements that should give them pause, for "ob gleich das Wunderbare eine der wirksamsten Springfedern ist, welche die Dichtkunst zum Interessiren anwenden kann, so thut es doch bei einem historischen Gegenstande keine gute Wirkung. Dieser fordert lichte Tageshelle: nur in der Wahl und Schilderung der Situationen, und in dem Ausdruck der Gefühle, kann bei einem solchen, Poesie angebracht werden. . . . Die Vermischung beider Gattungen aber giebt ein widerliches zitterndes Licht, — wie eine Illumination am Tage" [even though the miraculous is one of the most effective springs that poetic art can use for evoking interest, it has no good effect on a historical object. This demands the bright light of day: only in the selection and depiction of the situation and in the expression of feelings can one bring in poetry. . . . The intermingling of these genres, however, gives off a repulsive, trembling light — as artificial illumination during the day] (Braun S, 246). In other words, dramatists must use great care in not allowing the genres to bleed into each other. Merkel commends Schiller for his attempt and says that he would have succeeded had he not included the "Märchenhafte" [fairy-tale elements]. Despite his strong negative words about Schiller's contamination of one genre with another, he finds this play to be Schiller's most beautiful one thanks to the lyrical language and detail.

The anonymous review presented as a series of letters in *Neue Bibliothek der schönen Wissenschaften und der freyen Künste* from Leipzig, also dated 1802, continues to explore the notion of the romantic, disagreeing with Merkel's explanation as well as with that of another unidentified reviewer, by claiming that the romantic is born when imagination works its magic on history, covering the skeleton with flesh and skin. For this reviewer it is a simpler matter of giving a series of historical events a touch of fantasy, as one might decorate a table or a window. He claims that one finds a story "romanhaft" [novelistic] when the events fall within the realm of possibility, but the order in which they occur seems unreal. In *Die Jungfrau von Orleans* Schiller has included the historical events without providing a dramatic purpose that unites them and without putting them into logical (and thus, in this case, historical) sequence. These omissions render the play less realistic and less deserving of the term *historical*.

In 1803 a lengthy unsigned review appeared in the *Neue allgemeine deutsche Bibliothek* that chastised Schiller for not cleansing the historical material of all of its supernatural (and thus improbable or impossible) elements. The reviewer says that David Hume's account of the Joan of Arc story should have served as Schiller's model, for it went a long way in undertaking just such a cleansing. The reviewer then picks apart the apparent miracles — the changing of the wind so that a transport of foodstuffs came across the Loire river to the French troops, for example — and explains that there is no miracle about the wind changing or a ship arriving with food, for these are commonplace occurrences. The French sources are actually cognizant of the fact that these "wonders" are no wonders at all, that Joan of Arc had no desire to perform miracles, that the prophecies she made did not all come to pass, and that she was eventually wounded and taken prisoner. Because Schiller had worked with these documents, says the reviewer, he must have realized that these "miracles" were mere coincidences. There is a limit to what one will believe, and the Dark Knight, a ghostly spirit without reason or impetus for its stage appearance, transgresses this limit. This "miracle" is unbelievable, and Schiller has made a grave mistake in placing it on stage.

Die Jungfrau von Orleans puzzled critics to a greater extent than *Wallenstein* and *Maria Stuart*, partly because in this play, the miracles so unbelievable to the Enlightenment mind were part of the historical sources themselves. Was Schiller wrong to choose such material as a dramatic subject? What did he mean by "romantic tragedy"? The issues raised by critics of *Die Jungfrau von Orleans* dealt more with the questionable propriety of including "factual" and "fantastic" elements on the same stage than on the poet's right to mold historical materials to suit his artistic purposes.

Many of Schiller's contemporaries expressed admiration or even adoration for Schiller's late historical plays. His idealism, poetic talent, and perceived intentions were highly appreciated. Critics were aware of his introduction of historical inaccuracies; but most found this practice acceptable, primarily because Lessing gave poets the license to use such inaccuracies. At the same time, some critics alluded to the pedagogical advantage of portraying history onstage. The broad sweep of history was at stake, and many critics agreed with Schiller that art could give a more accurate picture of reality than reality itself. *Die Jungfrau von Orleans* baffled and annoyed critics, but Schiller's reputation, firmly established by the time of the play's appearance, gave him some latitude; critics tended to question their own assessment of the play rather than Schiller's skill or intent. In short, Schiller's technique of creating a poetic teleology on stage out of historical raw materials — fitting well with his belief in the notion of *Universalgeschichte* — found a positive reception from the majority of contemporary reviewers. After Leopold von Ranke and, especially, his "scientific" successors made their mark in German intellectual history, attitudes and tastes in regard to what was expected in a historical drama changed.

Notes

[1] To avoid confusion, "Braun SG" refers to Julius Braun's *Schiller und Goethe im Urteil seiner Zeit*, "Braun S" to his *Schiller im Urtheile seiner Zeitgenossen*. Both were published in 1882.

Works Cited

Berghahn, Klaus. "From Classicist to Classical Literary Criticism, 1730–1806," in Peter Uwe Hohendahl, ed. *A History of German Literary Criticism, 1730–1980.* Lincoln and London: U of Nebraska P, 1988, 13–98.

Braun, Julius, ed. *Schiller im Urtheile seiner Zeitgenossen.* Berlin: Luckhardt, 1882 [cited as Braun S].

———. ed. *Schiller und Goethe im Urteil seiner Zeit.* Berlin: Luckhardt, 1882 [cited as Braun SG].

Fambach, Oscar. *Schiller und sein Kreis in der Kritik ihrer Zeit.* Berlin: Akademie-Verlag, 1957.

Goethe, Johann Wolfgang von. *Kunsthistorische Schriften und Übersetzungen.* Berlin: Aufbau, 1970.

Heuer, Fritz, and Werner Keller, eds. *Schillers Wallenstein.* Darmstadt: Wissenschaftliche Buchgesellschaft, 1977.

Lecke, Bodo, ed. *Dichter über ihre Dichtungen: Friedrich Schiller von 1795–1805.* Munich: Heimeran, 1970.

Lessing, Gotthold Ephraim. *Hamburgische Dramaturgie.* In his *Lessings Werke,* vol. 6: *1767–1769,* ed. Klaus Bohnen. Frankfurt am Main: Deutsche Klassiker, 1985, 293–302.

Ludwig, Albert. *Das Urteil über Schiller im neunzehnten Jahrhundert: Eine Revision seines Prozesses.* Bonn: Friedrich Cohen, 1905.

Oellers, Norbert, ed. *Schiller — Zeitgenosse aller Epochen: Dokumente zur Wirkungsgeschichte Schillers in Deutschland. Vol. I: 1782–1859.* Frankfurt am Main: Athenäum, 1970.

Reill, Peter Hanns. *The German Enlightenment and the Rise of Historicism.* Berkeley: U of California P, 1975.

Sengle, Friedrich. *Das historische Drama in Deutschland: Geschichte eines literarischen Mythos.* Stuttgart: Metzler, 1969.

2: Hegel, Herder, and Ranke: Schiller during the Century of Historicism

AFTER 1800 FORCES were set into motion that gradually brought about a more detail-oriented focus in historiography. The shift was not complete until closer to mid-century, but the seeds were sown, primarily by J. G. Herder. While other thinkers, such as Wilhelm von Humboldt (1767–1835), Georg Wilhelm Friedrich Hegel (1770–1831), and Friedrich Schleiermacher (1768–1834) played a role in the shift, it was Herder who first successfully questioned *Universalgeschichte*. As early as 1774 Herder was rethinking his conception of history, the notion that every age should be examined in light of its own national and chronological conditions. For Herder history was a chain of events stretching through generations in manifold series of cause and effect but without a universal organizing principle. There was no progress toward a morally superior state, or greater freedom, or anything at all: history was simply "value-filled diversity" (Iggers, 30).

Within the historical stream, the nations were centers around which a specific kind of crystallization occurred. Herder is associated with burgeoning nationalism, as he was the first to examine nations historically; he thought that the historian's task should be to observe the dynamic movement within nations. Values are determined by the spirit of each individual nation, and, thus, for Herder poetry and art are always national and historical. "*Historismus*" (the term adopted for the new approach to history and historiography in the nineteenth century) initiated an awareness of the spectrum and diversity of human values. "In a certain sense, every human perfection is national, secular, and most closely considered, individual" (quoted in Iggers, 35), Herder claimed. Historicists believe in positive progress for mankind and in the ability of historians to understand history and reality, but they reject the notion of a teleological organization of history.

One may ask what happens to the role of the critic in this shift. The critical field around 1820 was too varied to give a single answer. The Romantics' cult of genius looked to the individual artist rather than to a community of critics to help form public opinion. Nevertheless, Herder, for example, saw the critic as a publicity agent for the writer, lifting up aesthetically worthy objects for contemplation by the public. In this way the critic improved cultural and political life. In this sense the critic is an Enlightenment product.

Herder was keenly interested in the development of drama. In particular, he studied the specifically German conditions that produced a Goethe and a Schiller. In accord with this thinking he viewed taste as historical, not universal. For Herder good taste, political freedom, and national consciousness are intertwined.

Humboldt agreed with Herder that collective forces are primary and that the nation is the best embodiment of such forces. The state attains paramount importance for him, as it does for Hegel and Leopold von Ranke. He moves Herder's argument forward and takes it on a different tack: there is no meaningful development in history. He subscribes to the possibility of the "genius," a notion that provides an explanation for many changes of historical direction and unusual events. He makes a claim for the role of the irrational in history, an idea especially important to nineteenth-century historians and one that made them even more wary of attempting to thematize or organize history. Humboldt's philosophy foreshadows Ranke's "scientific" method: first, one must make an impartial, accurate examination of events; then one engages in an act of comprehension, which cannot be performed through the intellect but must be achieved by intuition.

Although Herder takes credit for many ripples in historical thinking at the beginning of the "historicist century," Hegel remains the period's most influential thinker. His ideas on race drew attention away from individual progress and toward his theories of crystallization (though these ideas cannot be examined by current scholars without uneasiness about their eventual consequences). While Schiller and his contemporaries were aware of Herder's work, the criticism of Schiller's late historical plays from the years immediately following their appearance shows little evidence that Herder's ideas had yet had any influence on the perception of historical drama.

Hegel's *Lectures on the Philosophy of History* (1822–23) are the primary source for his theories about history. The nature of Hegel's project meant, however, that he spread himself over many fields of inquiry, and it is not an easy task to schematize his thinking. He viewed history as the progressive manifestation of the Absolute Spirit, a process that is entirely rational and comprehensible. In other words, history is ruled by reason. Peoples or nations take precedence over individuals in this process; in the Hegelian system "the individual becomes a means within a larger process" (Iggers, 40). While Hegel's ideas resonate with the category of universal history, his particular version has significant implications for nationalism.

Hegel's approach to literary criticism falls into line with his historical thought, not least in his promotion of national art. Hegel sounds like Schiller in valuing romantic art more highly than any other kind — although *sentimental* is the word Schiller would have used. Within romantic art, tragedy is the pinnacle. This ranking is partly owing to historical factors; according to Hegel, a culture must be at a certain point in its development before it can produce tragedy. The greatest flowerings of drama have occurred after great cataclysms in history (Hegel uses the example of Shakespeare's dramas coming after England's break with the Roman Catholic Church). Nevertheless, in what Gert Ueding calls a significant misunderstanding (222), Hegel was shocked by *Wallenstein*. Because death triumphs over life, he finds the play "nicht tragisch, sondern entsetzlich" [not tragic, but horrifying] (quoted in Ueding, 222).

The turn from examination of the broad context of history to the focus on individual facts and contexts played a major role in the discrediting of Schiller's historical writings, but the historical dramas were also reexamined in this light. The result, as one would expect, is a more negative critique of *Wallenstein*, *Maria Stuart*, and especially *Die Jungfrau von Orleans*.

It is, however, not only the new view of history that changes the reception of Schiller's dramas. Georg Büchner begins to write dramas that are heavily influenced by Schiller, but the idealism is not to be found. The portrayal of members of the lower classes moves into the spotlight in, for example, *Woyzeck* (composed 1836–37; published 1879) As George Steiner notes, "Woyzeck is the first real tragedy of low life" (274); his agonized spirit "hammers in vain on the doors of language" (275). Not only are issues of class difference brought into focus from a different perspective; issues of language and representation of reality are problematized in a way they are not in Schiller's plays.

Before considering Ranke's ideas in more detail, we will look at two pre-Rankean critics and how they judged Schiller's late historical plays: the poet Ludwig Tieck (1773–1853) and the editor of an early edition of Schiller's works, Karl Hoffmeister (1796–1844).

Tieck and *Wallenstein*

Albert Ludwig notes that the years 1815 to 1825, as attested by that famously huge bibliography of German literature, Goedeke's *Grundriß*, show a smaller number of publications concerning Schiller than any other decade of the nineteenth century. He attributes this fact to the negative view of Schiller held by most Romantics. Ludwig Tieck was among the most negative, although Josef Freiherr von Eichendorff (1788–1857), in his complaints that Schiller was abstract and rhetorical, went even farther than Tieck. Tieck made his mark not only as a novelist and short-story author of the Romantic school; his work as a literary critic was praiseworthy, as well as prolific. He came under fire from his contemporaries, however, for his harsh criticism of what he perceived to be Schiller's weaknesses. He finds *Wallenstein* a deplorable work. His primary criticism is that Schiller removes the hero's destiny out of its historical context instead of letting the two flow into each other. In this way Schiller moved away from Shakespeare, the perfect example, in Tieck's opinion, of what historical drama should be. In his 1826 review of *Die Piccolomini* he attaches some importance to the extensive research that preceded Schiller's composition of the drama. What is most striking, however, is that his review seems to be the first to attempt to place Schiller in a nationalist context. He lauds Schiller for choosing a subject from German history, claiming that there is no more noble poetic setting for the historical tragedy than one's homeland. He furthers this patriotic, nationalist theme when he speaks of the love of fatherland that the poet can inspire. The poet has a special gift for mirroring the historical process, which is a product of conflict and hardship. He becomes a prophet, a historian, when he embraces his material and creates a work in which the viewer can see both past and present. Tieck makes it clear that he is not speaking about the representation of individual events such as revolts or executions; he claims that what is considered a great moment is actually a vision that can only be perceived by one who is equipped with the talents of a seer. It is not accessible by the average person, and thus the poet needs to intercede. Further, if the poet becomes entirely absorbed in a historical event, it becomes greater and more poetic the closer it stays to the truth; the less the poet needs to discard inconsistencies, or what Tieck terms "spröde Bestandteile" [fragile components, 42], the more perfect the resulting work of art. Tieck claims greatness for Schiller because of the latter's mastery of form and understanding of the historical whole, comparing him favorably to Shakespeare; in addition, he ranks Schiller with the best of the historians for his understanding of the "big picture" of history. He also praises Schiller for allowing the profound bitterness and melancholy of the Thirty Years' War to surface in the dramatic work. He agrees with Schiller's assessment that the historical Wallenstein was poorly suited as a tragic hero and needed poetic assistance; Tieck thinks, however, that Schiller gives too many motives for the hero's downfall.

It seems to be important to Tieck that the play be credible. He mentions certain historical inaccuracies (Thekla's age, among others); nevertheless, in speaking of *Die Piccolomini* he claims that the audience believes everything and feels entirely transported into the times in question. He criticizes the scenes where, as he says, one can sense Schiller's purpose too clearly; one example Tieck provides is the goblet scene, where the lower-class characters take front stage to provide a history lesson. He expresses disappointment that Schiller did not write a play more supportive of patriotic feelings; in addition, he criticizes the love story between Max and Thekla because it clashes with what is truly historical.

Although Tieck differs from reviewers twenty years earlier in that he focuses on Germanness and the advantages and disadvantages of realism, he is not yet concerned with historical accuracy to the point that it becomes the central focus. (Goethe came to Schiller's defense in strong terms, going so far as to call Tieck pathological in his criticism, though Goethe was also one of the few contemporaries of Tieck who found his criticism to be of significance).

When the burst of Romanticism waned after the mid 1820s, Schiller's work began to experience renewed popularity. A return to political concerns took place after the July revolution in 1830. The continued covert work of the *"Burschenschaft"* [fraternity] movement — members of which were primarily students interested in political freedom and the unification of Germany — contributed to a new interest among young adults, in particular, who began to find the Romantics old and out of date. The increasing freedom of the press aided the growth of liberalism, and soon Schiller was tagged as a liberal. (Of course, this association was bound to rein in enthusiasm for him after 1848.) In addition, the publication of Goethe and Schiller's correspondence in 1830 did much to further Schiller's popularity. Even Grabbe, perhaps the finest writer of historical dramas after Schiller and Büchner, accorded Schiller respect; he sees in the return of Schiller's popularity a renewed blossoming of historical drama of a specifically German sort. In fact, he finds Schiller a better dramatist than Shakespeare, for the Englishman only created chronicles without a midpoint, catastrophe, and poetic goal. On the other hand, for the Germans he claims a desire for a treatment that is concentrated and dramatic as it renders the historical idea. Shakespeare may well excite a handful of aestheticians, but Schiller, because of his genuine and healthy German mind, created historical dramas that were far more valuable to Germans than the work of any foreigner could be.

Although Schiller was still popular at midcentury, the increased political activity of the 1840s pressed literary concerns into the background. Georg Herwegh, in his famous collection of political lyrics, *Gedichte eines Lebendigen* [Poems of a Living Man (1841)], could ask, "Was soll uns jetzt noch Schiller oder Goethe?" [What good are Schiller or Goethe to us now? (Ludwig, 51)] just as easily as others could claim Schiller's legacy as a political ally.

Tieck was able to identify aspects of Schiller's work that either heralded his waning popularity or contributed to it. As Ute Gerhard notes (758), he was sensitive to the dangers of selecting favorite lines from the plays and turning them into winged words, captions in family albums, and proverbs. This was, of course, precisely what happened to Schiller's dramas as the century moved forward.

Karl Hoffmeister

Karl Hoffmeister's mammoth biography and analysis of Schiller's works appeared in 1840. In his opinion, Schiller's work with the sources while writing *Geschichte des Dreißigjährigen Kriegs*, coupled with Goethe's influence, gave him the most historical- objective point of departure possible, using the "*Schicksalidee*" [idea of fate] as the ideal principle for his tragedy. For the first time, Schiller is able to progress from his earlier, more subjective-sentimental dramas to a true-to-life objectivity in which he can incarnate ideals in his stage characters. A criticism Hoffmeister makes regards the Max and Thekla story line; he sees this addition to the historical material as evidence that Schiller has not fully overcome a tendency toward sentimentality.

The transplantation of a subject from the fertile earth of freedom and history to that of the heart and the passions is the metaphor applied by Hoffmeister to *Maria Stuart*— in other words, we see the fruits of history in the play, but they have been removed from their roots. The presentation of the individual historical woman, Mary, Queen of Scots, is the main thrust of the tragedy, and all historical material has to conform to this task or be removed. As an example, Hoffmeister takes Schiller's omission of nearly any mention of Mary's son, King James VI of Scotland. The purpose was to protect his character, Maria, from any possible maternal patina. In addition, says Hoffmeister, Schiller has removed all outer trappings of her royalty — she never speaks to her people, for example. The critic also speaks of the alterations made in Maria's age, but not disparagingly. It is important to make her youthful, beautiful, desirable.

Hoffmeister uses Friedrich Raumer's *Die Königinnen Elisabeth und Maria Stuart* (The Queens Elizabeth and Mary Stuart, 1836) to examine Schiller's uses and abuses of the historical material. He notes that Schiller followed the sources available to him at the time that he wrote *Maria Stuart* but has problems with how Maria's death was motivated. Here he differentiates between "history," which Schiller did not follow, and the historical sources, which he did (256). He thinks that Raumer's historiographical contributions are and will remain the final word on the "true" version of the biography of Mary, Queen of Scots. He views the communion scene as yet another diversion from history, not because of the act of administering the sacrament itself, but because it makes clear to the audience that Maria felt free of guilt in the Babington conspiracy. Hoffmeister takes Elisabeth's side against Schiller, asking why he would put her right to the throne in question, and why he would permit her to act as an ordinary woman. Why would she sign the death warrant except to calm her people? Why would she hesitate to sign the death warrant when all of the lords and advisors voted for execution?

Hoffmeister eventually shows some annoyance at Schiller's reworking of the historical material, claiming that he has twisted, ignored, and added to history to a degree that makes *Maria Stuart* almost as unhistorical as *Don Carlos*. He points out other places where Schiller has ignored or consciously revised historical sources, including dates. He brings up the fictitious relationship between the imprisoned Maria and Leicester, the latter's departure for France, Mortimer, the meeting of the queens, and, by implication, everything that occurs in act 5. There are many more disparities, he says, in addition to the ones he has mentioned.

After this most thorough enumeration of the discrepancies — a more comprehensive list than any other critic had drafted up to 1840 — Hoffmeister turns to the justification for Schiller's having treated historical materials with such a free hand. Schiller was obliged to "do violence" to historical facts in order to transform a drama of world history into a passionate play about one individual. He quotes Raumer's misgivings about Schiller's tragedy: Schiller's play should have conformed more closely to the template of historical drama, according to Raumer. An indirect criticism of the harsh dialogue between the queens in act 3 can be detected: Hoffmeister claims that greater attention to "wahre" [true] history would have resulted in a more dignified and worthy tragedy.

Hoffmeister reminds the reader that Schiller is less interested in the historical partly because the subject matter, by Schiller's own admission, appealed more to his heart. There is, for example, no attempt to portray the court authentically (the attention to historical detail in *Wallensteins Lager* comes immediately to mind), "keine solche wahre Züge des brittischen Volkslebens, keine solche scharfe *historische* Charakteristik des Menschen" [no such true features of the life of the British people, no such sharp *historical* portrayal of the people's character] (276). Instead, Schiller is concerned with the portrayal of the individual, and it is partly this concern that led the playwright to say that he had to engage in a poetic struggle with the historical material.

Next Hoffmeister fires a salvo at H. F. Hinrichs, whose study of the relationship of Schiller's historical plays to their sources, *Schiller's Dichtungen nach ihren historischen Beziehungen und nach ihrem inneren Zusammenhange* (Schiller's Work in Relation to Their Historical Relationships and Their Internal Context) had appeared in 1837. He begins his polemic by remarking snidely that

Schiller's Work in Relation Neither *to Their Historical Relationships* Nor *To Their Internal Context* would have been a more suitable title. Hinrichs defends the fictitious meeting of the queens on the ground that this "unhistorical" presentation is in actuality historical because it provides an allegory for the power struggle between Catholics and Protestants during the time of the play. Hoffmeister claims that this is the most absurd thing one could say; these are not two queens if one is in chains. Hoffmeister points out that Schiller himself saw his play as not entirely devoid of pedagogical benefit. In addition, Maria herself knows English law, politics, and history extremely well.

Hoffmeister's final pronouncement on *Maria Stuart* is that Schiller has succeeded in uniting historical conditions — if one disregards the inaccuracies — with a picture of a woman. He claims that because of the play of emotions generated by the tragedy the audience either forgets the flaws or ignores them. His interpretation of Schiller's pronouncement about the moral impossibility of the scene between the queens is that in that case, the dialogue exceeded the boundaries of art; this is precisely the kind of flaw that Hoffmeister believes is negligible in the face of the effect produced in the audience.

Hoffmeister begins his analysis of *Die Jungfrau von Orleans* by referring to a historical account of Joan of Arc's life, Monsieur del Averdy's manuscript summary of 1790. We can, thus, anticipate that he will compare historical sources and Schiller's poetic product. Perhaps to soften the criticism, he notes that by using widely different time periods and geographical areas in his plays, Schiller did not choose an easy research path. Hoffmeister adopts the view that each of the historical plays takes Schiller one step further in developing a poetic form, but also one step farther from prosaic reality. At the same time, he claims that Johanna is less a "wonder" than her predecessors in his oeuvre: we never see the development of those other characters, but Johanna's character and mission are clearly developed on stage. Hoffmeister compares Schiller's Johanna to earlier idealistic characters, claiming for the latter a more subjective and lyrical cast; in this case, despite the unreal air around the historical Joan, Schiller has succeeded in giving his version of her a solid independence and a sharper delineation than, for example, his Mary, Queen of Scots.

After this introduction, Hoffmeister focuses on the historical inaccuracies. His first target is Schiller's use of the Virgin Mary as Johanna's divine intercessor rather than, as the sources tell, St. Michael and the Archangel Gabriel. This change, he says, was made to provide a dual meaning and a parallel for the term *holy virgin*. The next item is the number of visions: Schiller uses the "holy three" to draw a parallel to the Holy Trinity, though in reality Joan of Arc had many visions. Then he points out that according to the historical accounts, the maid had to prove herself in many ways before she was admitted to the court and allowed to lead men into battle; in the play she has already experienced military successes and need only prove herself by identifying the true Dauphin and telling him what he has dreamed. As he does in the case of *Maria Stuart*, Hoffmeister points out numerical discrepancies: Talbot, for example, died twenty-two years after Joan's death at the stake. The historical Joan claimed at her witchcraft trial that she had never shed anyone's blood; in the play she kills soldiers before the viewer's eyes — in fact, part of her vow prohibits her from sparing English lives. Hoffmeister sees this alteration of fact as a serious flaw (although it is not apparent why) but acknowledges yet again that Schiller need not adhere to fact; indeed, an onstage hero is required to carry a sword for dramatic effect.

Hoffmeister wonders how Schiller could find fault with Goethe for his operatic Klärchen in *Egmont* but include the equally fantastic Dark Knight in *Die Jungfrau von Orleans*. This is a Shakespearean tactic, and Hoffmeister acknowledges that Schiller's task is, after all, the dramatic shaping of the intrusion of heaven and hell into earthly matters (359). Attempting to analyze the appearance of the Dark Knight, Hoffmeister can only guess that he is a forewarning of Johanna's breaking of her vows.

While Schiller could have simply related the "true" history of his Johanna, ending with her burning, this would have resulted in an epic in dramatic form whose ending alone would have been tragic. Schiller instead wished to present a more complex kind of tragedy; Hoffmeister reminds us that Schiller has never chosen to portray a simple struggle with fate or with outside forces. History, as it has been read by Schiller, is merely too cut and dried.

Hoffmeister captures a significant difference between *Wallenstein* and *Die Jungfrau von Orleans* when he makes a distinction between lyrical and dramatic portrayal. He claims that the latter play presents the most sublime aspect of humanity dramatically — in *Wallenstein* it is lyrical — because he ties Johanna to her history and to particular religious beliefs; he no longer needs a special ideal character, as in *Wallenstein,* because he is able to create this miraculous character without removing her from the sphere of her gender or of history (375). In this way, argues Hoffmeister, *Die Jungfrau von Orleans* is more accurate in a historical sense. He disagrees with Wilhelm Schlegel's pronouncement that Shakespeare's account of Joan of Arc in *Henry VI,* though naturally colored by patriotism, is far more accurate than Schiller's, protesting that Shakespeare made her out to be a sorceress and a "leichtfertige Dirne" [girl of loose morals]. He quotes Karl Wilhelm Solger, who saw the play as an undramatic, impractical idealization of history that hovers in the air. Solger's main objection is that the miracles are unconvincing. Solger and Schlegel, says Hoffmeister, belong to the same artistic school, and they judge Schiller's play on the basis of a rigid and foreign conception of what a historical play should be and not on the basis of the material itself. Because this material is new, argues Hoffmeister, one should refrain from judging it by old standards. Solger and Schlegel are especially upset that Schiller's Johanna does not burn at the stake; Schlegel thought that the play would have been more moving had Schiller tinkered less with history. Hoffmeister counters this claim as well: Schiller had to invent a deep conflict within Johanna's soul in order to portray her true strength; had she been a mere empty vessel for God's mission, she would have been less moving. Her greatest virtue would have been patience, and in this respect, Hoffmeister alleges, she would have been a mere repetition of Maria Stuart.

Hoffmeister claims that the historical basis of *Die Jungfrau von Orleans* is not suitable for a drama. Nevertheless, Schiller succeeded in re-creating the spirit of the Middle Ages and in remaining within the bounds of a specific time, people, and religion. In this connection he mentions Schiller's poem "Das Mädchen von Orleans," written in reaction to Voltaire's bawdy "La Pucelle d'Orleans," which was well known and much recited in Weimar during Schiller's time. Hoffmeister points to this poem as a successful combination of the idealized Joan and the historical one and notes that Schiller has done more for the historical Joan than even Pope Kalixtus III, who pronounced her innocent.

Tieck and Hoffmeister return time and again to the ways in which Schiller creates characters who are, in essence, lightning rods for historical forces. They thus show their sympathy for the Romantic tendency to cultivate the individual. They are slightly more concerned about issues of historical accuracy than were Schiller's contemporaries, but they do not vitiate the plays in their entirety on such grounds. Both contend that poetic license holds sway in these matters. On the other hand, one can perceive the shift in the function of the critic: neither Tieck nor Hoffmeister mentions pedagogical matters.

Leopold von Ranke and Post-Rankean Criticism

Leopold von Ranke, "the founding father of German historiography," began his important work in the 1820s. He had been famous for ten years before his influence was established, for, as Lord Acton says, "the strongest men who came up were carried away by Hegel" (29). Ranke's work displays his roots in the religious and intellectual world of the Enlightenment; his attempts to unite the two opposing facets of historical work, narrative and detail, are reminiscent of Enlightenment attempts to do the same. Early on, Ranke expressed the desire to write "universal history," yet another connection to the Enlightenment. Although Ranke did not propose a particularly new approach to historiography, his fine narrative style and his concomitant attention to accuracy in using historical sources certainly contributed to his popularity. The most oft-quoted Rankean phrase, history "wie es eigentlich gewesen" [the way it actually was], has helped to sow confusion about his real project. People tend to associate Rankean historiography with an attention to detail devoid of theory or externally imposed order. In fact, Ranke insisted that examination of individual events is the only way to perceive an external order; this order, however, is beyond what the human mind can perceive. He owed much to Barthold Georg Niebuhr, who belonged to the Historical School at the University of Berlin. This school was in opposition to Hegel, because he viewed diverse phenomena as manifestations of a rational principle difficult for humans to perceive, while the Historical School believed that these phenomena comprised reality itself. Ranke thus found himself somewhere between these two positions.

Ranke is considered the founder of modern historiography not only within Germany but also internationally. With the entrance of Ranke onto the stage of historiography, history drops its teleological component and does not attempt to project a future. Ranke is not a universal historian because he does not believe that history consists of a linear moral progress; instead, he thinks that every age has something unique and valuable for the historian to study.

"Scientific history" has become the more popular term for the brand of German historiography founded by Ranke and others. Advances in other areas of inquiry, such as biology, chemistry, and physics, suggested the application of a scientific method to the study of history as well. Ranke has been falsely accused of advocating a purely "scientific" approach to history, when, in fact, he wished to uncover a unique methodology for a "human science of history" (Iggers & Powell, xiii), retaining the literary aspects of historical narrative while employing scientific methods in document research. Emphasis came to rest then on the observable rather than the deducible, and new ways of uncovering artifacts and documents were explored. Scientific history tended to look at the interworkings of great powers, using diplomatic documents, and this procedure led to an emphasis on political history.

Because mid-to-late-nineteenth-century Germany found itself in a time of political upheaval and reconfiguration after the Napoleonic era, historians were often involved in politics proper; one wonders to what extent this dual activity resulted in their theories becoming more pragmatic. After 1857 demands for unification were being presented, and a journal, the *Preußische Jahrbücher* (Prussian Yearbooks), was founded for this purpose; contributors included such historians as Heinrich Sybel, Heinrich Treitschke, Hermann Baumgarten, and Wilhelm Dilthey. These men were smitten with the same optimism about the nature of the state as Humboldt and Herder had been fifty years earlier. Like their Marxist counterparts (who will be discussed in chapter 5), they subscribed to an antitheoretical mindset. Going hand in hand with the notion of scientific inquiry is a rejection of conceptual thinking. More emphasis is placed on the historian's ability to assume the role of his or her subject, and intuition plays a great role for Ranke, as well as for Dilthey (see chapter 3). Perhaps because of his childlike faith in the moral quality of the state, however, Ranke essentially ignores the possibility that a political institution can abuse power. Literary critics, too, were drawn into political activity and often found themselves mouthpieces for Wilhelminian ideology. Criticism underwent a shift in two directions: some critics aligned themselves with the political goals of the ruling class, while others avoided politics in favor of egotistical expressions of their personal opinions about the texts. One can inquire as to extent to which Ranke's naiveté about the politics of the ruling class affected the former group.

After his death Ranke came under fire for having presented too narrow a focus by emphasizing the political over economic and cultural issues. He had used diplomatic and other political documents as sources and had ignored certain economic, social, and cultural artifacts. The historian Rudolf Vierhaus claims that Ranke was poorly informed about working-class conditions and social questions in general. But although Ranke fell into some disrepute, the historians who followed him for most of the nineteenth century remained focused on the issues he had brought to the fore. After 1870 historiography became even more scientific, leading Friedrich Meinecke to detect "a laboratory smell" (Iggers, 87).

Under such circumstances, one would expect Schiller's late historical plays to suffer under the lens of laboratory-oriented expectations. In the latter half of the nineteenth century Schiller's historical writings were often mocked; his plays were still accorded some leeway because of their poetic intentions, but Lessing's pronouncement seems to have been largely forgotten. It is easy to guess how Schiller, the poet of individual freedom, fared during a time when individual freedom faded into the background, while the ideals of unity, justice, and patriotic interest came to the fore.

Mid-century Critics

In 1852, four years after the failed revolution, Ferdinand Gustav Kühne gave a speech at the Leipzig Schiller celebrations in which he claimed that Wallenstein was a mirror of Napoleon Bonaparte. He compared them to meteors flying over a world that cannot understand them, and he tightened the connection between Napoleon and Wallenstein through a reference to one of Schiller's best-known aphorisms: "aber die Weltgeschichte blieb auch für ihn [Napoleon] das Weltgericht" [but even for him (Napoleon), world history became the world court (Oellers, 405)]. He accused both of murdering the revolutions that brought them to power and claimed that Schiller prophesied Napoleon's downfall in the tragedy. Here Schiller's Wallenstein is seen for the first time through an ominous lens. But the dramatist is not yet criticized for the way he misuses historical documents.

This criticism first occurs in a review by Otto Ludwig, who examines the trilogy in 1857–58 (*Shakespeare-Studien,* in his *Werke* 1908). He remarks first on the protagonist, whom he sees as absolutely flawed and weak. He calls Schiller's hero "unwahr" (untrue) and goes on to critique Schiller's use of historical sources. Ludwig obviously has expectations that Schiller's characterizations cannot fulfill because the poetic project takes precedence over historical accuracy. Gordon is seen as overly sentimental, and all the characters are utterly unhistorical; they are actors of Ludwig's time who have thrown on outwardly true but ultimately deceptive costumes from the inconceivably wild times portrayed in the play. He finds the astrological aspects an excuse for Wallenstein's actions, not an integral part of the play; and, above all, he criticizes Schiller's Wallenstein as "ein Zungenheld" [a hero of words] rather than actions. This hero, he claims, does not fully integrate historical and ideal aspects; the entire characterization is melodramatic. He even presses Schiller (whom he calls "our favorite writer") indirectly into patriotic service by asking how Germans are supposed to arrive at a proper understanding of history when the playwright confuses the audience by presenting such false idealism and sentimentality. To be sure, similar criticisms were made by a few of Schiller's contemporaries; but the important issue here is the overwhelmingly negative view of Schiller's deviation from historical fact.

The novelist Gustav Freytag follows Ludwig in criticizing Schiller's failure to adhere to historical facts. In a speech titled "Schiller und das Ideal," delivered in 1851 in Leipzig, Freytag seems to have felt differently, for there he praised Schiller's idealism, issuing from his heart and soul, as an antidote to photographic realism and cold formalism. In the essay "Zum dramatischen Bau des *Wallenstein*" (On the Dramatic Construction of *Wallenstein,* 1863), however, he claims that had Schiller followed the historical material more closely, he would have had a more historically accurate, poetically finer drama. Schiller should have shown how Wallenstein is led to commit treason instead of how he is indecisive in putting these treasonous feelings into action. For Freytag the most dramatic potential would have been realized had Schiller shown how the decision to commit treason had grown from the hero's own passionate soul.

René Wellek singles out Hermann Hettner's critical work as among the most impressive contributions to *Germanistik* in the nineteenth century. Hettner (1821–82) had argued against Hegel early on in claiming that art must always be subordinate to nature (primarily in his *Gegen die spekulative Ästhetik* [Against Speculative Aesthetics, 1845]). By the time he writes on *Wallenstein* he has developed as a critic, although Wellek finds it problematic that Hettner splits his expectations for content and style. Content, argues Hettner, is historical; style is not. This distinction sets up guidelines that Schiller is bound to disappoint; indeed, Hettner decries Schiller's "futile ambition of resuscitating the ancient tragedy of faith" (Wellek, 293) in the late historical plays.

Hettner is fervently interested in historical tragedy, and, as one might guess, he argues for a forward-looking content in which the pathos should be political in nature. He finds Christian Friedrich Hebbel one of the finest contemporary dramatists, primarily because Hebbel's plays to a great extent realized Hettner's program — contemporary content based on ideas, with nothing left to chance.

It is not surprising that Hettner devotes a portion of his *Geschichte der deutschen Literatur im 18. Jahrhundert* (History of German Literature of the Eighteenth Century, 1856–70) to *Wallenstein*. Besides his criticism of Schiller for adhering to what he perceives as ancient content, he is also, like his contemporaries, critical of Schiller's historical inaccuracies. Even so, Hettner was a supporter of the Enlightenment. (Hettner's work on the Enlightenment and on classicism is among his finest.) According to his analysis, Schiller sins against both economy and clarity of exposition in the name of aesthetics, flaws so egregious that they render the piece unproduceable. After pointing out that the plot suffers from the most severe improbabilities, he claims that Goethe himself could not refrain from implying that the fabric of *Die Piccolomini* was "verwirrend künstlich und willkürlich" [confusingly artificial and capricious] (letter of March 9, 1799, in Hettner, 511). Perhaps most heinous of all, however, is Schiller's negligence in regard to the historical underpinnings. Hettner claims that Schiller had to denigrate the historical Wallenstein in order to allow the strange series of events to take the stage as "fate." He admits that the state of historical research on Wallenstein in 1870 means that the general's plans remain unknowable; he criticizes Schiller, however, for filling in the gaps and for believing that he could ascribe these gaps to Wallenstein's character. Whereas the unsigned reviewer in *Allgemeine Literatur Zeitung* could assign the filling of historical gaps to the poet, eighty years later the poet is chastised for doing so. Of course, Hettner could be complaining subconsciously about what was used to fill the gaps, for Wallenstein appears to him a pitiable figure, a dismal Hamlet who is brave in planning but cowardly in action. Though it becomes difficult to trace Hettner's argument — to follow whether it is the historical or the Schillerian Wallenstein that he has in mind — it becomes clear that the critic finds Schiller's "improvements" on the historical materials contemptible. Hettner does temper his criticism by claiming that Schiller makes up for some of the flaws of *Die Piccolomini* in *Wallensteins Tod,* where Wallenstein rises again in dignity. Surprisingly, Hettner ends by saying that while the play's flaws should not be hidden, *Wallenstein* is, on the whole, the greatest German play.

J. G. Rönnefahrt wrote a series of individual studies of Schiller's major plays in his series *Blätter aus der Naturgeschichte der Menschheit* (Pages from the Natural History of Humanity), an ambitious project detailing the appearances of manifestations of the "Geist der Zeit" [spirit of the times]. First, in 1859, he turns his attention to *Die Jungfrau von Orleans.* After apprising the reader of the public's enthusiastic reception of the drama, he moves into a discussion of the two opposing concepts: the "romantic" and the "tragic." Equating tragedy with antiquity and the adjective *romantic* with the Middle Ages, he urges the reader to accept the apparent paradox of viewing the form as tragic but the content as romantic. Schiller is able to fuse these two, says Rönnefahrt, because the "romantic" is so objectively portrayed that the viewer cannot imagine that history occurred in any other way.

Rönnefahrt sounds like a true historicist when he avers that the deeds and decisions of people in medieval times must be measured by other yardsticks than those appropriate for Schiller's or the critic's time. Later in the article, however, he describes the period in strongly negative terms, claiming that human rights and freedoms had been "exterminated" and that the church and the patriarchy were the few oppressing the many. He goes on to say that historians describe the period subjectively; he who is able to differentiate between objective history (to which, one infers, Rönnefahrt has special access) and subjective history (that which is written by the historians) will appreciate Schiller's depiction of Joan of Arc, because her world is presented in the "objectivster Objectivität" [most objective objectivity] (34), as Rönnefahrt tautologically expresses it. He says that contemporary Romantic literature has a tendency to obfuscate, swoon, and soar; Schiller's drama, however, displays none of these qualities but, rather, depicts them; the poet himself stands above them.

While sounding, on the one hand, like a historicist, on the other hand Rönnefahrt praises Schiller's ability to bring out the "allgemeinmenschlich" [universally human] in his characters. He allows Schiller the privilege of changing history to suit his purposes; the play is, however, so successful at putting an "objective" account on stage that the audience cares just as little about Schiller's intent as it does about the historical Joan. Rönnefahrt sees her as a personage who has raised herself above the majority of people, who allow the influence of historical changes to pass over them without effect; she is, thus, one of the historical individuals who wander along the peaks of life. These individuals contribute to the "Geist der Zeit" (6); the masses are either influenced by this spirit without knowing it, or they try to work against it consciously. Johanna's father does not want her to assume such a position but to remain in her place in the masses. Rönnefahrt reminds us again that the play is set in the Middle Ages, and that it typifies a medieval mindset; we should not then be surprised to see wonders on the stage, because they are realistic within this mindset.

Rönnefahrt begins to sound like a Marxist critic when he discusses the role of the masses, whom he seems to be chastising in the previous discussion. He mentions Dunois's status as a bastard and says that this status does not bother him, but he reminds us that those of lower classes would not have enjoyed the same privileges; impoverished mothers of bastards were put in the stocks, for example. Johanna, though emerging from an unprivileged class, breaks through the restrictions of her age in order to carry out a specific purpose. She is free in a higher sense of the word than freedom of action: she frees herself from her desires and passions to follow a higher purpose. This notion follows the medieval ideal of religious sacrifice, but she works for the fatherland as well as for God. Besides, she represents the people. Rönnefahrt draws political conclusions related to the French Revolution but stops short of advocating democracy.

In a section clearly arguing against Herder's ideas Rönnefahrt paints the play as having antinationalist overtones. He equates Johanna's fall from grace, her wandering in the forest, and her eventual triumphant return with the people's temporary seduction into blind nationalism. He even connects the Black Knight with this interpretation. Finally, the sacrifice of Johanna (the people) at the end marks a return to the fold, for it is the banners of the king that are sunk over her body. This ending, too, is better than reality, because Schiller shows how Joan was eventually reinstated and canonized. This tragedy, Rönnefahrt summarizes, is an example of Schiller's desire to perfect the one great idea underpinning all of his work: the idea of an "ächtmenschliches Staatsleben" [truly human citizenship]. Schiller looks at every one of world history's footsteps to find traces of the path that humans must walk to find true dignity.

Rönnefahrt's next paper deals with *Maria Stuart*. Here he returns to the importance of the masses in history and says that while the audience gets a foretaste of this importance in *Wallensteins Lager* by seeing soldiers from the lower classes displaying their potential power onstage for the first time, it is brought home securely in this play. Elizabeth, after all, complains about the onerous burden of constantly serving the people; she acknowledges their importance, however, and, indeed, Schiller implies that she is willing to sign the death warrant because they demand it. Rönnefahrt takes this idea one step further and sees a religious notion of mankind beloved of God. He returns to his idea of humans struggling toward their determined goal; this struggle, he claims, is "Naturgeschichte."

Rönnefahrt points out that what takes place in *Maria Stuart* — the execution of a queen because of the judgment of people, not of her peers — is a new event in the history of the world, and that this regicide is the subject of the play. The personal fight of the queens leads to world-historical consequences; but primarily, this event (the death of Mary, Queen of Scots) and the Reformation itself grew out of the spirit of the times. The principle of Protestantism is the emancipation of the individual, claims Rönnefahrt, and this emancipation is what Schiller is portraying. In its ultimate consequence, it can lead to such tragedies as the murder of royalty.

Through murdering her peer, Queen Elizabeth has shown how regicide can be justified, not least through the command of the subjects of another country. This tragedy is one to which all of Elizabeth's subjects contribute. Rönnefahrt goes so far as to call it a "Menschheitstragödie" [tragedy of humanity] (22), in which humanity destroys itself before the throne of world justice. That which is most tragic is — in reference to Schiller's pronouncement that world history is the world court — that the defendant is all of humanity. Rönnefahrt sees this self-destruction of humanity happen in the meeting of the queens. Maria represents the world-historical tendency toward ennobling; Elizabeth, on the other hand, is "herzlose Selbstsucht" [heartless selfishness] (23), a force that leads to isolation and despising of others. Schiller brings this situation to crisis, therefore, in the attempt to show the nature of humanity by the use of an individual example, one that for people in the nineteenth century is especially interesting because they are still living in the shadow of that outcome (Protestantism).

Rönnefahrt then critiques Hoffmeister, reiterating the latter's objections to Schiller's ignoring of historical details and his ultimate judgment that Schiller was not writing historical dramas. As in his study of *Die Jungfrau von Orleans,* Rönnefahrt takes the tack that Schiller, in ignoring, reorganizing, or rewriting those details, has actually stayed truer to history than even the most "objective" historiographer. He compares Schiller's play to two historical works, F. E. Schlosser's *Weltgeschichte für das deutsche Volk* (World History for the German People, 1844) and F. A. Mignet's *Geschichte der Königinn Maria Stuart* (History of Queen Mary Stuart, 1851). (One would like to have heard Rönnefahrt's motivation for using sources that Schiller would not have had at his disposal; perhaps his point is that Schiller somehow knew what had really happened.) He says, for example, that Schlosser portrays Sir Paulet as much stricter, much rougher, and more ruthless than he was in reality; Schiller keeps Paulet an honest and somewhat sympathetic sort. One can ask how Rönnefahrt would know what the real Paulet was like. The critic now builds a careful case regarding Maria's guilt in the murder of her husband. He points out Schlosser's reference to Elizabeth's letter, saying that she would agree to meet Mary only after she had justified her actions in this regard.

Rönnefahrt draws our attention to the physical space of *Maria Stuart*. It begins in a private room; in the sixth scene the "Weltgericht" [world court] enters this private space. The critic perceives Mortimer not as a fictitious figure but as a composite of Babington and other conspirators. He calls up examples of "unhistoricity" and explains why they are used in the dramatic genre, saying that they are not unhistorical at all: the compression of time, for example, he explains as a recitation of dialogue that has elsewhere only appeared in written form. The task of drama is to show the spirit of the times, the meaning behind the events, the urges of the soul that push people into action. This task is accomplished in "charakteristischen Zügen" [characteristic lines] (43).

Occasionally it is unclear whether Rönnefahrt is directing his comments at the historical figures or at Schiller's characters. But when he speaks about the differences between the two types, he becomes more lucid. The most significant difference between the historical Mary and Schiller's Maria lies in the question of Mary's/Maria's guilt. The historical Mary was guilty of inciting resistance to Elizabeth; for Schiller's purposes she would not be a tragic figure, because she would be receiving the punishment she deserved.

In Maria's relationship to Leicester, Rönnefahrt sees Schiller's technique of bringing together many complicated threads that would have taken too much time to explain in a drama — the story of Mary's earlier engagement to him and Elizabeth's envy of Mary's beauty, to name two. In addition, Schiller lends Leicester a certain shimmer, a dignity that he does not deserve historically, in order to honor Schiller's sense of poetics. Maria receives similar treatment. It is not unhistorical in her case, however, because Mary was able to charm the entire world; men were willing to die for her, sight unseen, just on the power of the rumors of her beauty. To create this effect onstage, Schiller needed to compensate. Rönnefahrt claims that Maria is a poet because of her sensuous, captivating charm; Elizabeth is her exact opposite and can only approach the hearts of the audience by means of her physical juxtaposition with Maria. For this reason, Schiller needed to resort to poetic and historical untruth. Along these lines Rönnefahrt asks whether Schiller has been too harsh with Elisabeth, who, after all, was one of the most praised and powerful of England's rulers. Inasmuch as it is the poet's task to show what goes on beneath the surface of history, he is justified in so doing, because, according to Rönnefahrt, "insofern charakterisirt nun die Heuchelei und Verstellung der Elisabeth einen Zustand des ganzen Zeitalters" [Elisabeth's hypocrisy and falseness characterize the entire age she represents] (65).

Next Rönnefahrt turns to Schiller's purpose in fabricating the meeting of the queens. To represent the individuality that the Reformation enabled, he needed to personalize the reasons for the execution of Maria, and to do so most effectively, he had to have the women meet onstage. Dramatically, this scene is one of the most wonderful creations of the stage. "Der historische Kritikus" [historical critics] (74), says Rönnefahrt, protest against it. But what the queens tell each other has been said in letters, he notes. He cites his historical sources to show the increasingly insulting tone of the letters and that it became clear that the women hated each other. On the question of Schiller's pronouncement that the meeting was morally impossible, Rönnefahrt explains it as an issue of whether or not Elizabeth would ever have allowed such a meeting voluntarily. He goes on to relate their dialogue to greater historical principles: the meeting of antiquity and modernity, particularly in relation to notions of freedom and individuality. Maria represents the modern, individualized human being, because her motivations are personal: she does not recognize the absolution of her early sin but continues to perform a personal act of repentance; she refuses to recognize the commission set up by Elisabeth; she attempts, through connections with Leicester, to secure her freedom.

Rönnefahrt says that Schiller connects the outcome of the queens' meeting with Maria's eventual execution for dramatic purposes. Following his logic, we can see that this move makes explicit Maria's hand in her own downfall and thus makes the play more tragic. In addition, Rönnefahrt sees this tactic as incarnating his belief that historical events are set into motion by acting individuals. The queens temporarily shed their roles as political figures and become mere women at the meeting. This transformation ties in with the Reformation: it would not have occurred had it not been for acting individuals such as Martin Luther. Here too, Schiller shows how, during the course of the Reformation, morality replaced belief as the principle governing human behavior.

Rönnefahrt ends his study by claiming for Schiller the status of the artist most able to portray human nature in a truly realistic fashion. He shows humans in the way God made them, in the divine truth of their being, on their way through freedom and fate to eternity. His efforts as a critic are difficult to categorize. He clearly believes that a historical play should transmit accurate historical information. It seems, however, that he is bending over backward to argue that Schiller was doing so, even in the case of the clearly unhistorical meeting of the queens. He seems to subscribe to a Hegelian view of history in his choice of the term "Naturgeschichte der Menschheit"; yet, at the same time he agrees with Schiller's notion that history is determined by individuals.

The novelist Theodor Fontane reviewed *Die Piccolomini* following a performance on November 11, 1871. In condescending tones he lauds the play for its idealism, though he is quick to point out that it is not advisable for such plays to be performed all the time. Instead, there should be a place where one can go to receive such idealistic nourishment, "das befreiende, das erhebende Wort" [the liberating and elevating word] (22:1, 88), a place like a church — the implication being that it is there for those special occasions when one needs it. It becomes clear from Fontane's review that Schiller's popularity has already waned, that Schiller has become passé; but he believes that a Schiller renaissance is in the offing. He exhorts modern playwrights to devote themselves to examination of Schiller's craft and to be witness once again to the power of the word.

Sixteen years later Fontane reviewed another production of the trilogy, given over the course of two evenings in May; his review bears witness to a shift in critical focus. His first concern is how important historical accuracy of costuming and similar physical concerns have become in the preceding ten years. He claims that the authenticity of the soldiers' costumes, be they Tiefenbachers, Holkische Jäger, Walloons, or Pappenheimers, seems to be the main issue at stake. There are questions, too, about the authenticity of the scenery: Fontane reports that gold and black were used effectively but that their use generated doubts in his mind about their appropriateness to the time; here he refers to recent studies on how the scenery would have looked during the Thirty Years' War. He says that the costumes of the harquebusiers did not seem to fit the play; if they *were* authentic, he says, he would have preferred them to be inauthentic. In regard to *Wallensteins Tod* he makes similar comments about the stage backdrops. The play itself thus receives less commentary than does its staging. It is possible that Fontane, reflecting a general feeling of the time regarding not only Schiller's outmodedness but also the faded glory of the historical drama, believed that Schiller's play needed no further comment.

Helene Raff published an article on Schiller's Max in 1929; I bring it into the discussion at this point because it is a summary of several articles from the 1870s regarding possible real-life prototypes for Max Piccolomini. She begins by referring to the nature of Max, an "invented" character; indeed, according to historical sources, Octavio Piccolomini married only *after* he became "*Fürst* [Prince] Piccolomini." Attempting to trace a possible historical model for Max, Raff refers to articles by Freiherr Arnold von Weyhe-Eimke (1870), the Italian E. Piccolomini (1871), and Theodor Paur (1874 and 1876). All of these articles rely heavily on archival documentation; Raff goes to a source ignored by them, Franz Christophs von Khevenhüller's work with the unwieldy title "Conterfet Kupferstich (so viel man bekommen können) denjenigen vornehmen Ministern und hohen Offiziers So vor Kaysers Ferdinand des Andern Geburth an bis zu desselben seeligsten Hintritt continue und successive Ihrer Kayserl. Majestät gedient" [Engravings of likenesses (as available) of those noble ministers and high-ranking officers, from before the birth of Emperor Ferdinand II until his death, who have served this imperial Majesty]. This work was published in Leipzig in 1722 and was known by Ranke. It is the life story of the historical Wallenstein's cousin Max von Wallenstein; Raff speculates that Schiller used this figure as the model for his Max Piccolomini because of the many points of contact between the two. Not only is the conflict of allegiance similar, but the personality of this Max is similar to that of his dramatic counterpart.

Raff goes on to report on Ranke's "Geschichte Wallensteins" [History of Wallenstein] (1869), a study that refutes some of Khevenhüller's points. She cites several detailed examples and, in turn, the documentation used by Ranke himself either to point out inaccuracies in Khevenhüller's work or to introduce findings made since 1722. This Max never wavers in his loyalty to the Kaiser, despite his sponsor Wallenstein's plans. After the summaries of Khevenhüller's report and Ranke's subsequent work, Raff concerns herself with sources that Schiller may or may not have used, including the *Annales Ferdinandei* (which he mentions himself) and the *Conterfet*, which, she claims, the libraries in Jena and Weimar own and probably did during Schiller's time. Nevertheless, despite extensive evidence for Khevenhüller's thesis, Raff claims that this historical model was only useful to Schiller tangentially; certain personality traits and Max Piccolomini and Max von Wallenstein's conflict over loyalty to the emperor and to Wallenstein appear in the drama, but little more. Max von Wallenstein did not possess the intense pathos of Schiller's Max; rather, he was forced into compromises that Max Piccolomini never would have considered. Raff does, however, point to the tragic nature of the historical Max von Wallenstein; the fact that his comparative passivity may rob his figure of the aura surrounding heroes even on the downward slope does not make them less noble (178). This thorough engagement with historical documentation found its beginnings in the 1870s; Raff uses a similar method to examine the relationship of Schiller's creation to its historical model nearly sixty years later.

In his *Dramaturgie der Classiker: Lessing, Goethe, Schiller, Kleist* (1882) Heinrich Bulthaupt agrees with many of his century-mates that the *Wallenstein* trilogy is Schiller's finest dramatic work, but he tempers his pronouncement by pointing out that it did not give Schiller the popularity of a Shakespeare. He examines reasons for this disparity and draws the conclusion that the Thirty Years' War is not the kind of historical background that incites enthusiasm. He points to the difficulty of retaining artistic perspective when dealing with subject matter so painful from a national standpoint; because of this very difficulty, he thinks Schiller allows the historical spirit to emerge from the massive drama more clearly than it does in any tragedy by Shakespeare. He scolds those who would complain about Wallenstein's monologue that they do not appreciate greatness of Schiller's type — that a country sees such a genius at the most once every 300 years.

Bulthaupt sees *Maria Stuart* less as a historical drama than as a story about women's pride and weakness, but he exhorts directors to pay attention to proper costuming and actors to deliver the lines naturally, not bombastically, for the latter destroys the "historischen Geist des Stückes" [historical spirit of the play] (268). In general, Bulthaupt is less concerned about historical accuracy than his predecessors. For example, he mentions the historicity of Burleigh's secret suggestion to Paulet to allow Mary, Queen of Scots to be murdered but sets it aside with the words "nebenbei bemerkt, der auch geschichtlich den Wünschen der Elisabeth entsprach" [by the way, it also was Elizabeth's wish] (271). Bulthaupt discusses Mortimer, but not because he lacks a historical counterpart. Two pages later another reference to historicity is set in parentheses: "NB ungeschichtlichen" [Note: unhistorical] (273). Here Bulthaupt is pointing out that Schiller fabricated Maria's surrender of her designs on the throne; he does not criticize Schiller for doing so.

Bulthaupt's analysis of *Die Jungfrau von Orleans* begins, surprisingly, with the declaration that Schiller is being proved to have been historically correct as more and more research is done into the background of Joan of Arc, even though he invented more in this story than in any of his other historical dramas. Bulthaupt goes on to explain that because Schiller was mainly interested in the maid's ideals, his portrayal had to show that side of her, and this interpretation has proven to be correct: she was infused with patriotism as much as with divine inspiration. Bulthaupt sees in Schiller's almost androgynous characterization of Johanna an accurate rendering of a nonsexual girl-child, although she is able to perform feats that most men cannot. He says that Schiller is usually so rational and "echt historisch" [genuinely historical]; in this case, however, he could not remove the wonder from the play because he believed in the wonder himself. Why did Schiller not choose to follow the historical material more closely, asks Bulthaupt, when it would have given material for one of the most crushing tragedies imaginable — Johanna alone and discredited after her glorious accomplishments? Perhaps Schiller was not emotionally capable of doing that to a heroine who had grown so close to his heart. Bulthaupt ends by reminding the reader that Schiller himself mentioned three possible endings for the play — a piece of information that critics first discuss in this period, although it was Böttiger who made the claim.

In his *Schiller's Wallenstein* (1886) the Austrian scholar Karl Tomaschek introduces *Wallenstein* as a direct product of the dramatist's prior historical work on the *Geschichte des Dreißigjährigen Kriegs*. In reviewing Schiller's earlier piece he refers directly to the permissible historical approaches of his own day, claiming that to imply that Wallenstein has committed treason directly after his dismissal at Regensburg, or even earlier, was "nach dem heutigen Stande der historischen Forschung . . . nicht mehr gestattet" [according to the current-day conditions of historical research no longer permitted]. It is curious that he uses *gestatten* [permit], a verb which implies that there are rules to follow in regard to historical method. Tomaschek avers that according to recent research, Wallenstein's negotiations with the Swedes and Saxons were actually permitted by the emperor (4). After chiding Schiller gently for daring to fill in the historical gaps with his own theories about Wallenstein's behavior, Tomaschek admits that Schiller mentioned that no one at his time had found any documentation to prove why Wallenstein committed treason (Tomaschek notes that no such documentation has been found since). In less gentle tones Tomaschek accuses Schiller of gleefully indulging in the negative aspects of Wallenstein's character that he found in his allegedly one-sided sources and using them in his historical writings. To Tomaschek it is shocking that Schiller behaves as an artist even in his historical writings. Even though one must banish any thought of artistic freedom in historical writing, at least this freedom assisted Schiller to escape from the barriers of the historiographer; it permitted him to open up the heart of his hero Wallenstein. Returning to Schiller's admission of the confusion surrounding the historical Wallenstein, Tomaschek accuses Schiller of wanting a *possible* Wallenstein and not a real one, "der zugleich dem Herzen näher stehen soll" [that at the same time is supposed to be nearer to one's heart] (14). Of course, Schiller had said that he wished to portray not "real" but "probable" historical characters on the stage. Here we can trace a Rankean concern for accurate interpretation of documentation. Tomaschek says that because of his aesthetic beliefs, influenced by Johann Joachim Winckelmann and Lessing, regarding the ugliness of extremes, Schiller was obliged to moderate the historical Wallenstein's barbarity and wild nature. To make the play a successful tragedy, the hero had to excite a sympathetic response in the audience, and thus the dramatic Wallenstein was fitted with positive characteristics. Some critics, says Tomaschek, saw these alterations and wished for a fully heroic Wallenstein, one who had peace of mind. In response to them Tomaschek states that such a portrayal would stand outside the trilogy entirely and would signal a return to the time of *Die Räuber* and other earlier works. Tomaschek represents a true post-Rankean critic who, nevertheless, has some sympathy for flexibility in the treatment of historical documentation for poetic purposes.

Heinrich Düntzer, the most prominent of the Schiller critics in the 1880s, wrote a series of studies on dramatic works that he published in *Erläuterungen zu den Klassikern* (Commentaries on the Classics, 1886–1908). Included are volumes on the *Wallenstein* trilogy, *Maria Stuart,* and *Die Jungfrau von Orleans.* These studies all follow the same pattern: sections on the genesis of the play, the source materials, and the contemporary criticism, followed by a scene-by-scene analysis that constitutes the bulk of the study. This "scientific" arrangement mirrored the need for scientific forms and demanded a comparison of the play to the historical materials. Düntzer sees Schiller's modifications in a negative light.

In the volume on *Wallenstein* Düntzer summarizes the historical sources, including Schiller's own essay and the discoveries made since Schiller's death. Because Düntzer is one of the few critics who also pay close attention to historical materials in *Maria Stuart* and *Die Jungfrau von Orleans,* we will concern ourselves with these two plays.

Düntzer begins his analysis of *Maria Stuart* by positing the difficulties of presenting the various attempts to liberate the Scottish queen and pointing to Schiller's contrary purpose: to show Maria's acceptance of her death as atonement for her involvement in the murder of her husband, Darnley. To achieve this end, Düntzer says, Schiller needed many "Um- und Zudichtungen" [rewritings and additions] (92). Among the discrepancies he mentions are the compression of time and the meeting of the two queens. In his analysis of *Die Jungfrau von Orleans* Düntzer gives the genesis — in which he is careful to quote Schiller's comment of 24 December 1800 on this play: "Das historische ist überwunden, und doch, so viel ich urteilen kann, in seinem möglichsten Umfang benutzt" [The historical has been overcome, and yet, as far as I can tell, utilized in its [broadest] possible range] (20) — and contemporary commentary and moves on to a treatment of the historical materials. Düntzer finds it germane that Schiller had considered a second version of *Die Jungfrau von Orleans* that would have been more historical than the first. The unreliable Böttiger, says Düntzer, went so far as to tell of Schiller's plans for *three* versions; this claim, however, is not supported by Schiller's papers or letters. Düntzer proves in this volume, as in the preceding ones, that he has undertaken thorough research, even citing the dates when Schiller returned volumes of historical materials to his lenders.

The first issue Düntzer takes up in his analysis of *Die Jungfrau* is a historical one: why did Schiller change the end of Joan of Arc's life so drastically? He asks, quite pointedly, whether Schiller was not obliged to keep the true ending. He brings up the question of tragic dignity, which would have been impossible to portray in a death at the stake. He suggests that Schiller could have chosen to have Johanna return home with her family after the coronation; in this case the ending would have been more modest, but it would also have stayed truer to the sources. Turning to the invented love story that proves to be Johanna's downfall, he defends Schiller from charges of historical inaccuracy by claiming that the playwright has simply given her a different source of guilt from those found in the historical sources.

Düntzer lists at some length instances where Schiller has taken liberties with his sources, often comparing how accurately Shakespeare followed history in writing *Henry VI*. He writes about the places where Schiller either accelerated the action or omitted explanatory material, citing questions of dramatic economy or character development. For example, had Schiller included all of the events that took place between Johanna's grasping of the helmet in Domremy and her appearance at court, Düntzer maintains, the latter would not have made such a compelling impact on the audience. While enumerating other instances that stem directly from the sources, he mentions that Schiller invented Johanna's prophecy of the death of Count Salisbury. Düntzer justifies the omission of the wife of Charles VII, Marie de Anjou (the play gives the impression that he is unmarried) and the ruler's younger age by claiming that a passionate relationship with his mistress, Agnes Sorel, makes the weak and indecisive king more sympathetic to the audience; it would have been difficult for him to provoke sympathy, however, if he were seen as a mere adulterer. Schiller also replaced the entirely unsympathetic historical courtier La Tremouille with the more accessible Du Chatel because, according to Düntzer, doing so makes the reconciliation scene between the Duke of Burgundy and his father's murderer more remarkable. In the course of explaining the impossibility of showing every battle on stage, he outlines exactly where the French and English camps lay in relation to each other. Coming to the entirely unhistorical Lionel, Düntzer speculates on the source of his name. He then deals with the issues of whether or not the historical Joan took part in hand-to-hand combat and whether the poetic Johanna should have done so. According to Düntzer, Johanna had to promise to kill her enemies without mercy in order more effectively to break two of her vows later, when she both falls in love with a man and fails to kill him.

Düntzer shows how several characters (the Archbishop, for example) differ from their historical counterparts but gives no reason for the difference. In addition, he notes that the Bastard first receives the name Dunois in 1439, eight years after the historical Joan's death. Düntzer, like Hoffmeister, mentions the anachronistic demise of Talbot. He remarks that Schiller had no use for the events that took place between May 8 and July 16 in the play. Was Schiller supposed to include *everything,* one wonders? He returns to this idea when he discusses what happened historically between act 1 and act 2, between act 2 and act 3, and so on.

The critic spends some time on the historical Joan's loss of credibility with the French. He concludes that Schiller was justified in creating a fictitious darkening of her soul to match the historical darkening of her reputation. But he asks, nevertheless, who the Dark Knight is, suggesting that the figure may be nothing more than a projection of Johanna's dark thoughts. Düntzer thus moves in the direction of psychologizing Schiller's Johanna, an interpretation that will be more thoroughly explored in the twentieth century.

Düntzer points out that some of Johanna's actions are historically accurate: carrying the banner before the king, kneeling next to him in the cathedral, the encounter with her relatives following the coronation, and her imprisonment. Everything else, he points out, up to her death is "freie, sehr glückliche Dichtung" [free, successful poetry] (106). He says that Schiller had the right to transport the audience into the times during which Joan walked the earth. His summary of the play is that it is a freely poeticized representation of the medieval legend of Joan but not a historical drama. He warns against trying to see the play in a political way, as a story of the liberation of the French people. He claims that Schiller had no intention of reminding his audience of the oppression that was at that moment being visited on them by Joan of Arc's descendants. Düntzer does not believe that Schiller was dreaming of a unified Germany under a powerful emperor. In support of this argument Düntzer cites Schiller's poem "Der Antritt des neuen Jahrhunderts" (The Beginning of the New Century) as evidence that Schiller harbored no such hopes but, rather, complained that the urge to power displayed by both the French and the English robbed the world of any hope of peace.

Although Düntzer plainly shows his admiration for Schiller's dramatic projects, the issue of how faithfully historical sources were followed preoccupies the scholar to the point that one feels that he is almost apologizing for Schiller. The thorough exposition of the historical reports and the repeated comparisons of these materials with Schiller's renditions creates a tension between the work of art and the materials on which it is based that nearly cancels the praise accorded him.

The nineteenth century follows Schiller in circles. There is an ebb and flow as his idealism is admired, then his lack of attention to historical detail is criticized. Toward the end of the century there is a feeling that critics wish to praise him, but the praise sounds pale and forced. Perhaps there is some perceived need to keep this icon in its place, and a reluctance to pull him off his dusty shelf completely.

The anniversary year 1905 brought Schiller celebrations, but they were only an echo of their counterparts in previous years. A renewed examination of Schiller took place, but its thrust was essentially political. Debate broke out between the Social Democrats and other leftists (see chapter 5) who claimed that the German bourgeoisie were paying homage to him in a sort of thoughtless sacrificial worship. They accused bourgeois critics of superficial regurgitation of prior criticism, while Schiller's true project was designed to benefit the proletariat. On the bourgeois side, Schiller's alleged alliance with the proletariat was stringently denied; instead, the focus was on Schiller as a champion for freedom and the individual. Still others wished "die mit Schiller mögliche Integration der verschiedensten sozialen Schichten und Gruppierungen zu realisieren — vom reformfreudigen Adligen über Unternehmer und Dichter bis hin zum Industriearbeiter" [to realize the integration, made possible with Schiller, of the most varied social classes and groups — from the reform-friendly nobility to entrepreneurs and poets to industrial workers] (Ute Gerhard, in Koopmann, 771). But this optimism was never realized. In 1905 Schiller had become more of an icon than a voice, and although his plays were occasionally staged, they had become worn and were not reevaluated in any meaningful way. In less than ten years Germany would experience "the war to end all wars," a devastating cataclysm that jarred every aspect of German life and society.

Works Cited

Acton, Lord. "German Schools of History," *English Historical Review* 1 (1886): 7–42.

Bulthaupt, Heinrich. *Dramaturgie der Classiker: Lessing, Goethe, Schiller, Kleist*, vol. 1. Oldenburg: Schulzesche, 1882, 244–92.

Düntzer, Heinrich. "Schiller's *Maria Stuart*," in his *Erläuterungen zu den Klassikern*, vols. 19–20. Leipzig: Wartig, 1885, 92.

———. "Schiller's *Jungfrau von Orleans*," in his *Erläuterungen zu den Klassikern*, vols. 50–51. Leipzig: Wartig, 1884, 106.

———. "Schiller's *Wallenstein*," in his *Erläuterungen zu den Klassikern*, vols. 17–18. Leipzig: Wartig, 1881, 127–59.

Fontane, Theodor. *Sämtliche Werke*, vol. 22: 1–2. Munich: Nymphenburg, 1964, 87–95, 119–20, 271–72, 467– 69, 665–68, 685–93, 745–47, 750–52, 893–96, 915–18.

———. *Sämtliche Werke*, vol. 22:2. Munich: Nymphenburg, 1964, 53–57, 286–89, 334–39, 470–85, 494–96, 554–61.

Hegel, Georg Wilhelm Friedrich. *Hegel on Tragedy*, ed. with an introduction by Anne and Henry Paolucci. New York, Evanston, San Francisco, and London: Harper & Row, 1962, xi-xxxi, 1–96, 112–24.

Hettner, Herman. *Geschichte der deutschen Literatur im achtzehnten Jahrhundert*, vol. 2. Berlin: Aufbau, 1961, 537–49.

Hinrichs, H. F. W. *Schillers Dichtungen nach ihren historischen Beziehungen und nach ihrem inneren Zusammenhang*. Leipzig: J. C. Hinrichs, 1837.

Hoffmeister, Karl. *Schiller's Leben, Geistesentwicklung und Werke in Zusammenhang*, vol. 4. Stuttgart: Balz, 1840, 8–72, 251–87, 317–84.

Iggers, Georg G. *The German Conception of History: The National Tradition of Historical Thought from Herder to the Present*. Middletown CT: Wesleyan UP, 1983.

———. and James M. Powell. *Leopold von Ranke and the Shaping of the Historical Discipline*. Syracuse NY: Syracuse UP, 1990.

Koopmann, Helmut, ed. *Schiller-Handbuch*. Stuttgart: Körner, 1998, 771.

Ludwig, Albert. *Das Urteil über Schiller im neunzehnten Jahrhundert: Eine Revision seines Prozesses*. Bonn: Friedrich Cohen, 1905.

Oellers, Norbert. *Schiller — Zeitgenosse aller Epochen: Dokumente zur Wirkungsgeschichte Schillers in Deutschland*, vol. 1: *1782–1859*. Frankfurt am Main: Athenäum, 1970, 158–77, 398–406.

Raff, Helene. "Wallensteins Max," *Westermans Monatshefte* 73, no. 146 (1929): 173–78.

Raumer, Friedrich. *Königinnen Elisabeth und Maria Stuart: Nach den Quellen im britischen Museum und Reichsarchive.* Leipzig: Brockhaus, 1836, 256.

Rönnefahrt, J. G. *Blätter aus der Naturgeschichte der Menschheit. Drittes Blatt. Schiller's romantische Tragödie: Die Jungfrau von Orleans.* Leipzig: Dyk, 1859.

———. *Blätter aus der Naturgeschichte der Menschheit: Viertes Blatt. Schiller's Trauerspiel Maria Stuart.* Leipzig: Dyk, 1861.

Schulte-Sasse, Jochen. "The Concept of Literary Criticism in German Romanticism, 1795–1810," in Peter Uwe Hohendahl, ed. *A History of German Literary Criticism, 1730–1980.* Lincoln and London: U of Nebraska P, 1988, 99–177.

Solger, Karl Wilhelm. *Vorlesungen über Aesthetik.* Darmstadt: Wissenschaftliche Buchgesellschaft, 1969, 621.

Steiner, George. *The Death of Tragedy.* New York: Knopf, 1961.

Tieck, Ludwig. *Kritische Schriften,* vol. 3. Leipzig: Brockhaus, 1852, 37–62.

Tomaschek, Karl. *Schiller's Wallenstein.* Vienna: Carl Gerold's Sohn, 1886, 1–38.

Ueberweg, Friedrich. *Schiller als Historiker und Philosoph.* Leipzig: Reissner, 1884.

Ueding, Gert. *Klassik und Romantik: Deutsche Literatur im Zeitalter der Französischen Revolution 1789–1815.* Munich and Vienna: Hanser, 1987, 222.

Wellek, René. *A History of Modern Criticism, 1750–1950: The Age of Transition.* New Haven and London: Yale UP, 1965, 182–229.

———. *A History of Modern Criticism, 1750–1950: The Later Nineteenth Century.* New Haven and London: Yale UP, 1965, 292–319.

3: The Metaphysical Crisis, the First World War, and the Aftermath

THE BELIEF — or, rather, the certainty — that human history is essentially knowable and logically explicable came under serious attack in the 1890s. The ideas of Friedrich Nietzsche, Sigmund Freud (1865–1939), Fyodor Dostoevsky (1821–81), and others began to call into question the existence of an objective cognitive force either within the individual or outside in either the physical or nontangible world. Instead of asking how one was to represent or retell history, one asked if it was possible to do so objectively at all. The limitations of human knowledge began to be acknowledged, and the ability of the human mind to comprehend historical processes completely cast into doubt.

Nietzsche ranks among the most prominent of the voices that began to dismantle historicism. In several of his works, particularly in "Vom Nutzen und Nachteil der Historie für das Leben" (About the Uses and Disadvantages of History for Life, 1878), he calls history into question and points out the cracks in the edifice of historicist thinking – indeed, in German Idealism in general. He claims that it is the arrogance of the technological-scientific trend as much as historical experience that has been guilty of undermining the formerly secure structure. While Nietzsche's infamous indictment of the study of history gives little reason for optimism about the meaningfulness of occupying oneself with the past, it did not cause thinkers to cease occupying themselves with it. If anything, a new series of impulses were directed at the representation of the past, either in protest against or in agreement with Nietzsche's ideas. With the failing reverence for history, the historical drama simultaneously lost its glow. In fact, it took on a distinctly negative tinge.

Before the turn of the century Neo-Kantians such as Wilhelm Windelband (1848–1915), Heinrich Rickert (1863–1936), and Wilhelm Dilthey were attempting to return to Kant, placing philosophy once again as the metasystem encompassing both the

"*Naturwissenschaften*" (natural sciences) and the "*Geisteswissenschaften*" (sciences of the spirit — history, sociology, and ethics, to name three). Windelband tried to develop a system of universal values; Rickert used transcendental logic to correct what he perceived as flaws in Windelband's paradigms but was attacked for ignoring the fact that human beings exist in history; Dilthey used the fledgling study of psychology in forming his own brand of Neo-Kantianism. While other thinkers were, understandably, focusing on the outward aspects of human life during this time of turmoil — that is, on the social and political ramifications of their theories — Dilthey looked inward. He did not subscribe to the state-oriented view of history/society that his predecessors did. Instead, he argued that individuals do not create a homogenous group. One cannot claim to know the individual through knowing a gathering of people to which he or she belongs, be it a political party or a family or a race. The individual will always hold back something that the group will never own. And so, no matter how deeply the state may reach into the life of the individual, it can never know or subordinate the entire individual. We will return to Dilthey, for he will provide an important perspective on Schiller's plays, not least in his lengthy study of *Wallenstein*.

The economic, political, and social upheaval left in the wake of the First World War can hardly be exaggerated. While the artistic fruits of the Weimar Republic are astonishing and now legendary, political unrest and economic instability led to disillusionment and cynicism despite the ecstatic blooming of the arts. The cataclysmic events left traces as diverse as rampant unemployment and absurd inflation rates on the economic front, and a continuing radical rethinking of historicist theories on the philosophical. The defining word during this time was *crisis*. Among the most vocal in this rethinking after the war was Oswald Spengler.

Spengler's notion of the cyclical nature of human history and the succession of self-contained, disparate cultures recalls Herder, but it is a dark echo. Civilization, as Spengler understands it, is the petrified stage of senility a culture reaches before its demise. Western civilization is thus for Spengler a dark time, and the title of his main work, *Der Untergang des Abendlandes: Umrisse einer Morphologie der Weltgeschichte* (The Decline of the West: A Morphological Sketch of World History, 1922), reflects the dire pessimism of his view. To be sure, the First World War and the economic and social misery it left in Germany provided fertile ground for such a view. The only vital force Spengler finds in Germany after the war is the urge to colonialize, to appropriate materials from more vital cultures; he calls this period "the age of Caesarism" (Heller, 183). Human freedom is an illusion; mankind merely follows its destiny in a world where individual action plays a minor role. The members of such a society are in possession of a sterile spirit and are incapable of creating.

For Spengler, the divide between facts and interpretation closes. Facts *are* interpretation, for the selection of facts is an act of interpretation in itself. In other words, the historian loses all hope of objectivity even before he or she tries to establish causal connections. Historical pictures can only be established by historical imagination, not by scientific reason. The tangle of cause-and-effect has blinded historians to the true impetus of history, "for no order can even emerge unless we discover how *all* things in history are related, not merely one to the other, but to something else: to a constant, a crystallizing principle" (Heller, 192). Spengler here sounds remarkably like Herder, while seeming to advocate a universal history, an explication of the interrelatedness of the entire scope of history. Spengler's telos, however, is not situated at the end of an uphill climb, the product of human progress; for him the end point is the end of civilization. There is no such thing as progress, and the only heroic act imaginable is courage in the face of complete historical relativism.

Writing two years after Spengler (whose theories achieved swift popularity), the theoretician Karl Mannheim (1893–1947) advocates a different view. Mannheim speaks, surprisingly, of a climate of utopia. He, too, speaks of a return to Kant and points to a demarcation of difference between the natural sciences, which tend to speak in generalizations, and history, which is individual and concrete. In other words, one needs to emphasize the difference between static science, on the one hand, and dynamic history and social science, on the other. The results of historical and sociological inquiry are personal and dependent on the individual perspective of the researcher. Mannheim calls into question in yet another way the possibility of the historian's objectivity. All historians are vulnerable to preconceptions not obvious to them. But in his view this is a positive development, for it grants to the individual a certain autonomy and importance.

Dilthey was among the first to follow Nietzsche's lead in posing questions about the meaningfulness of the study of history and the efficacy of scientific methods in researching it. Writing in the mid-1890s, he is included with Freud and Max Weber as members of the vanguard against positivism. To outline the situation broadly, Dilthey and others reacted against the moves made by Herder and Ranke and considered, even advocated, a move back to an altered notion of *Universalgeschichte;* in any case, and most importantly for our purposes, they had come to the conclusion that the scientific method fell short when called into the service of the study of history. While there was pessimism about the damage that the "arrogance of science" had done, there was also optimism about the scientific advances made through the preceding century.

Dilthey, writing in 1895, had less influence on historians proper than on historians of literature and art during his time; the former began to examine Dilthey only after the First World War because his work was not widely circulated until after his death. Dilthey's ideas are original while at the same time reflecting a wish that Schlözer had expressed over a century earlier: to unite an overarching system with attention to details. To this end Dilthey draws in human imagination and claims that an individual cannot understand history until he or she can relive it in the imagination. He points to the example of the conversion in the New Testament of Saul of Tarsus, later Paul, in whose mind Jewish law, pagan world consciousness, Christian faith, and his own conscience were fighting. Here historical forces from diverse periods came into contact with each other, and a transformation occurred. This example of Paul gives a good indication of Dilthey's mysticism.

Dilthey is important for our purposes because he was both a historian and a literary critic. He remained virtually unknown during his lifetime, however, and it is difficult to know when and how widely his writings were disseminated in Germany. His theories about history are summarized by Patrick Gardiner: "all physical expressions are expressions of mental events, or states, and the job of the Understanding (which is a faculty as well as a process) is to link up any given expression with its appropriate mental event or state" (211–12). In other words, Dilthey is interested in a process that synthesizes reason and history. Further, he pleads for the independence of literary works from their authors, for the intrinsic value of the aesthetic expression. In this way he is a Romantic, as well, advocating aesthetic immanence.

It is reasonable to surmise that accurate historical detail became less important to critics after the demise of historicism. One can ask whether Schiller experienced a renaissance of interest because of this change; the answer is complicated by the introduction of Schiller into German classrooms, but gradually, despite individual critics' laudatory and sometimes empty remarks, the dust collecting on schoolroom shelves reflected a forgetfulness about Schiller. To be sure, he was a canonical author whose importance was acknowledged, but true reevaluations were few. By the time of the Weimar Republic, whose cultural climate looked to the new and the daring, Schiller's concern with antiquity, idealism, and human freedom sounded naive and anachronistic. In the 1920s, however, Schiller experienced a small-scale resurgence in popularity. Examined here are critics who represent the trajectory from the 1890s – a period characterized by dissatisfaction with the "scientific method" — through the Spenglerian pessimism of the 1920s.

Dilthey's writings on the history of the German spirit, composed in the 1890s, were collected and published under the title *Von deutscher Dichtung und Musik* (On German Poetry and Music, 1933). (One should bear in mind that Dilthey did not have a chance to finish them, and at times it is difficult to follow his train of thought.) The importance Dilthey places on Schiller as a figure in the German spirit is evidenced by the fact that an entire chapter is devoted to him. Even in the introduction, Schiller's significance for Dilthey is articulated: he calls Schiller and Shakespeare two masculine leaders in the spirit of German poetry. These poets are seers, a word that connotes an importance that goes beyond the merely rational. Dilthey finds them to be representatives of human life, moved by relations between humans and fate.

As Dilthey writes about Schiller's reputation during the 1890s, he intimates the ways audiences have changed since the dramatist's time. He speaks of Schiller's continuing popularity on the stage, not only in Germany but in all the theaters of Europe; this popularity, however, concerns not Schiller the classic playwright but rather Schiller the innovator. Dilthey writes that while Schiller does not meet audience expectations because of something alien in form as well as in content, one does get something unexpected from his dramas. He is a great writer, claims Dilthey, and a renewed interest in Schiller will occur when the spirit of the times is more hospitable. In other words, Dilthey thinks that the audiences of the 1890s see Schiller as alien to their time, even though they can detect his genius. He sees *Wallenstein* not only as Schiller's best play but also as the beginning of modern historical drama. He devotes a few pages to this genre, claiming that Schiller devoted himself to "die großen Objektivitäten der geschichtlichen Welt, die über sein eigenes Privatleben ganz hinausreichten" [the great objectivities of the historical world, which went far beyond his own private life] (348). From the material he took from history, Schiller created a drama of ideas through his own imagination (this word so important to Dilthey) and through the inclinations of his own soul. This challenge, claims Dilthey, is the greatest one that can be made to the imagination: the envisioning of what *could* be, of what lies outside the borders of the conditions of our lives. Once one goes beyond these borders, one sees the possibility of change, and this vision is what makes Schiller's dramas modern: the realization of one's ability to affect the outcome of history through the imagining of a greater sphere (in this respect Dilthey anticipates Brecht). Dilthey, however, claims that this understanding of a great objectiveness is bound together with an assertive progression toward the ideals of the future. Here he attempts to reconcile individual efforts in the shaping of history with an awareness of ideals that will shape the future.

Dilthey goes on to describe Schiller's technique: the dramatist is entirely focused on the structure of his play, a structure that allows the action to accelerate gradually up to its final moment. He compares the imagination used in Schiller's plays to the imagination displayed by great historians who create strongly affective scenes, arranged to point to a strongly affective ending, and all bound together with a system of causalities. Each scene must perform two functions: it must be critically important to the system of causalities, and it must develop an internally passionate content. The former function is a historical, the latter a poetic one. It is the latter aspect that allows the poet to form historical materials to his/her use. Dilthey points out that Schiller is accustomed to working in antitheses in his philosophical writings; it is not surprising that his dramatic technique reflects this tendency. Schiller structures his plays around antitheses that are ideally and historically delineated.

Dilthey remarks that Shakespeare's dramatic development is psychological, whereas Schiller's is not. Rather, Schiller's is a conflict in words, a rhetorical fight that displays the confrontation of ideals. Dilthey, as other critics before him, refers to Lessing and traces the abrupt changes in Schiller's dramatic art to him; specifically, he points to how Schiller uses the atmosphere of place to lend his plays a greater historical power. In other words, we have come back to the attitude prevalent at the beginning of the century: that historical accuracy may be subordinated to the service of art. Dilthey sees Schiller's project as a unification of the deepest understanding of history with original power. Within this project he outlines three types, the first of which are the dramas of historical antagonism. Here the characters are representatives of historical forces, and this he sees as Schiller's true innovation in the genre of historical drama. In this category he places both *Maria Stuart* and *Wilhelm Tell*. The second category is the drama that describes the historical position of the protagonist and the world situation that becomes the fate he cannot overcome. In this category he places *Wallenstein*. This drama is deeper and more difficult because the conflict resides not only within history but also within the psyche of the protagonist. He discusses the technical difficulties for the historical drama in particular: for example, these plays generally have a lengthy development, which is impossible to render onstage if one is to produce the play on one evening. (Dilthey is obviously referring to *Wallenstein* here.) What is more, there is a need to represent not only the egotistical forces of great personalities but also the impersonal historical powers that determine the course of history, including the fundamental conditions of the people and their active ideas.

Dilthey's next remarks are reminiscent of the split the Neo-Kantians were attempting to resolve: the origins and laws of the historical drama that issue forth from *Geschichtswissenschaft*, the "science" of history, are justified by the relationship of this *geschichtlichen Wissenschaft* [historical science] to *der historischen Wirklichkeit* [the historical reality]. The critic goes on to explain that if there were some assurance that historical sources were entirely and dependably true, there would be no need for historical drama or fiction. Since people often fail to tell the truth, however, either because there are other motives in force besides a moral compulsion to tell the truth (political, economic, diplomatic) or because they remember incorrectly, credibility is a meaningless notion. *Wallenstein* tells the historical truth that is not to be found in the source documents. Rather, it is located in "wirtschaftlichen Verhältnissen, Veränderungen der Verfassungen, Machtbeziehungen der Staaten, dem Gegensatz der Richtungen und dem Verhältnis der leitenden Persönlichkeiten zu diesen Kräften im Ganzen und Großen" [relationships of commerce, changes in the constitution, power relations between states, the opposition of (political) directions and the relationship of the leading personalities to these powers on the whole] (381). Although Dilthey does not recognize the importance of the common man or woman in this summary of what constitutes historical truth, he penetrates to those areas that are most likely to give rise to attempts to prevaricate. These areas are not suitable for direct recording of events but need the power of a spiritual vision, something that always retains an element of subjectivity.

Dilthey turns next to this relationship between the historian and the artist. He claims that the historian becomes an artist when he attempts to represent intellectual and spiritual connections between the character of people of one epoch and another or great personages in their most intimate emotional or spiritual relationships to one another. Dilthey wishes to encompass moral issues here, as well. He compares the task of the historian to the task of the poet in relationship to historical material, viewing the way poets see such material as different from the way historians perceive it. They are on opposite ends of a scale, and between them stand the chronicler and the biographical artist (Plutarch is an example of the latter category). These figures in the middle are similar to the artist in that they have an interest in the anecdotal, the personal, the fateful. Historiography, however, is focused on establishing causal relationships, in creating a historical continuum out of single events. Dilthey says that Schiller's new contributions are his way of seeing historical objects poetically and his ability to place them into moments full of expression. Schiller is able to interweave the historical character with the historical milieu, something that even Shakespeare did not do, for, according to Dilthey, Shakespeare was unaware of different historical layers. (This point can, obviously, be argued, especially in light of recent New Historicist studies on Shakespeare.) Schiller was also Goethe's superior in this respect, for Goethe focused (especially in his *Egmont*) too little on the historically determined time frame of his plays. Part of Schiller's success lies in his ability to represent a historical totality that causes the beauty of individual details to retreat before it. This task demanded drama on a large scale and explains Schiller's need to expand the *Wallenstein* material into three dramas rather than presenting it in one.

Now Dilthey focuses on *Wallenstein,* the play that obviously lies closest to his heart. He introduces the play as an attempt to untie the knot of one of the most complicated historical personages against the backdrop of historical forces wrestling with one another. In this regard, Schiller's initial work with the sources (his *Geschichte des Dreißigjährigen Kriegs*) was essential. The Prologue, besides providing an arena for shielded reference to contemporary political events, sets the conditions for the audience's belief in the protagonist. Dilthey agrees with Schiller that the figure's historicity is a necessary condition for belief in the character's greatness. If this character is to engage the audience dramatically, it must evoke both historical and personal interest.

As a side issue – one that is clearly more interesting to our time than to his — Dilthey speaks briefly about the characters along gender lines. He claims that men are historical and make history, while women are unhistorical, naïve, and naturally perfect; this dichotomy pervades all of Schiller's plays. One wonders why Dilthey failed to notice a glaring exception in Countess Terzky, not to mention in the pair Max-Thekla. Max in his failure to create history seems to belie Dilthey's assessment.

Dilthey discusses Max and Thekla in connection with Schiller's basic concern with humanity. This concern, the need to interweave humanity into the historical portrait, explains Schiller's invention of their relationship. It is also indicative of a concern with moral standards that are applicable to the ideal human. As Dilthey notes, Schiller provides in Max and Thekla a yardstick against which the other characters are measured. So Max and Thekla are, as elsewhere, seen as representations of the Ideal; but Dilthey appends the belief in their necessity in a historical sense, as they provide the ideal that is present in history as opposed to an ideal existing outside of historical experience.

Dilthey gives a detailed account of the historical background of the play. Following this exposition, he turns to the characterization of Wallenstein, speaking first about the notion of the "*Herrschernatur,*" the person (almost always male) who seeks power not only for what it can procure but also for its own sake. In this play Schiller has gone further in examining this type than Shakespeare did; to do so he uses the concept of power as creative ability. Wallenstein is a perfect example of such power. Schiller generally uses transcendental idealism as a means of understanding practical genius, which is intimately tied in with creative ability, and he employs this technique with Wallenstein. He crosses the borders of the aesthetic conception of genius when he uses this basic determination of transcendental philosophy in the practical world: Wallenstein, abandoned by the greatest part of his army, finds within himself the creative ability that has already commanded an army out of nothing (399). Wallenstein transcends his own dire situation to reflect on his creative ability, a power that has raised him high and has now brought him into the most harrowing of situations. Dilthey says that what makes Wallenstein a historical character is the connection of qualities that are determined by a historical situation and are only to be understood by means of that situation.

A characteristic that other critics had seen as a grievous character flaw rendering Wallenstein unsuitable as a tragic figure is, Dilthey points out, actually an aspect of the character that makes it historical. For during the Thirty Years' War, Dilthey maintains, hesitancy and moving troops back and forth were common military strategy. He connects this military strategizing with mathematics, claiming that a calculative aspect is appropriate to the seventeenth century. He therefore finds the character Wallenstein, as well as the play, worthy of tragic treatment and goes one step further to call it even more historical than other subjects because of this alleged "flaw." The fact that this was Kepler's time, as well as his homeland, makes the mathematical connections even more historically appropriate.

The critic moves on to explore another historically appropriate theme of the trilogy: the belief in astrology, which is connected with the other mathematical aspects. This system is, to Dilthey's mind, even more historical. Through Schiller's notion of transcendental philosophy, the astrological aspects refer back to the deepest reaches of consciousness. Dilthey finds it perfectly understandable that astrology would take on such an important role in an age of mathematical calculation. The connection between politico-military genius and astrological belief is made possible by means of a mysterious tunnel that history itself has burrowed out. Finally, Dilthey ties this matrix, through his notion of transcendental philosophy, to a consciousness of the universal context of all of nature, a context in which Max and Thekla also find the basis for their spiritual unity. Max and Thekla serve as the common man; Wallenstein is the rational, calculating mind that sees other humans as numbers, as possible usable objects, as means to his ends. Ironically, because he sees them in this way he *mis*calculates in evaluating Buttler's and Piccolomini's loyalty to him.

Dilthey sees the words Thekla speaks as she resolves to journey to Max's grave, "Das ist das Los des Schönen auf der Erde" [Such is the fate of the beautiful on earth], as a philosophical phrasing of the vulnerability and ephemerality of ideals in this world. In this way Schiller strengthens the philosophical consciousness of the meaning of the world through giving his ideal characters the ability to thematize their suffering. Dilthey returns to a comparison with Shakespeare, claiming for him a historical consciousness of the context of life. Both Shakespeare and Schiller are able to present an entire historical world according to its causal conditions and to teach us to understand the historical world in all its manifold antagonisms. (Here, for the first time, Dilthey speaks directly about a pedagogical function for art.) One such condition is that there exist heroes who become fateful not only for themselves but also for the entire world.

This play thus becomes more "historical" than history itself. Dilthey says that the connections he has mentioned occur in history because history is entirely human. In this regard he speaks of Ranke's essays, of which the most compelling aspect is that they occasionally allow glimpses of such pieces of history, places where its complete humanity comes through. Such glimpsing is normally only possible through a poet, says Dilthey. In this sense Ranke was heir to Germany's poetic epoch. It is through humans that history should be represented in the present, the way Schiller has done it; historical ideas are impossible to represent abstractly.

After over thirty pages devoted to *Wallenstein*, Dilthey spends one page on *Maria Stuart*, the play that most closely reflects Schiller's historical sources. He does not even mention *Die Jungfrau von Orleans* but spends some commentary on *Die Braut von Messina*, *Wilhelm Tell*, and *Demetrius*. His comments on *Maria Stuart* reflect a different strategy, for it is a different type of historical drama than the *Wallenstein* trilogy. He views Maria as an authentic representation of the way of thinking and the education of the French court during her time. He also sees Mortimer in this light, as a product of the intrigues of Cardinal Guise. He summarizes that here, too, as in *Wallenstein,* the historical age and the historical character are chained together indissolubly.

Dilthey spends little time dealing with the historical inaccuracies that so bothered some of his predecessors, although he expends considerable effort relating the details from historical accounts. In some ways, he has more in common with Schiller's contemporaries; his reviews, however, bear witness to a struggle for synthesis. He wishes to prove that Schiller provides a new way of seeing and representing history, a way that relies heavily on the structures of consciousness and the interconnectedness of detail and grand design.

Although Dilthey was writing during a span of years ending in 1905, the work did not receive broad circulation until 1933. His ideas reflect a turning away from scientific views of history, but he does not embrace *Universalgeschichte.* Rather, Dilthey has found his own way of synthesizing elements of Rankean historiography, Hegelian dialectics, and psychological interpretation in a mystical, somewhat eclectic fashion. Dilthey is one of the greatest and most unconventional thinkers of the twentieth century, and his interest in Schiller, as well as his pronouncements about historical drama in general, would surely have had some effect on early twentieth-century criticism had his writings been distributed more widely at the time of their appearance.

At the beginning of the twentieth century — a time that saw an increased interest in class struggle and labor issues as Germany continued to industrialize — one group of critics continued to follow a line of positivist thought. One of them, Fritz Strich, published his *Schiller: Sein Leben und sein Werk* (Schiller: His Life and Work) in 1912. Characteristic of Strich's stance is a seemingly thoughtless adoration of Schiller. Leftist scholars would attribute such a stance to a general decline and demoralization of literary critics under a capitalistic and imperialistic system that made them spokespersons for the ruling class. Although Strich falls under the heading of "adoring scholars" — an attitude that remained popular well into the century — his book is worth examining. It includes a section on each of the three dramas we are examining, but like most other critics he spends more time on *Wallenstein.* Before turning to this play, however, he speaks of Schiller's novellas and sounds suspiciously like Dilthey. Describing novellas Schiller wrote during his hiatus from drama, Strich claims that Schiller wrote them as a historian of the human soul, and for that reason he was able to give them the appearance of historical truth. It is difficult to know, however, exactly what Strich means by this claim. When speaking of *Wallenstein* Strich discusses realism and says that Schiller planned to use it to make up for a flawed idealism. However, "die Aufgabe wurde dadurch schwerer und interessanter, daß der eigentliche Realismus den Erfolg nötig hat, den der idealische Charakter entbehren kann" [the project became more difficult and more interesting because actual realism needs the success that the ideal character can do without] (341–42). One wonders what kind of success Strich means here — political? Strich claims that the thorough study of historical sources was crucial to such a project, for Schiller needed to create the action, as well as the characters, from within their locale and time. According to Strich, he looked in the same sources he used for his *Geschichte des Dreißigjährigen Kriegs* in order to limit himself, a discipline that that allowed his ideas to be determined and brought forth by the environment and conditions of the seventeenth century. Strich speaks of the song at the end of *Wallensteins Lager* not as a piece of realism but as an audible symbol of the unity of Wallenstein's troops: the act of singing unites voices of all ranges, qualities, and timbres. But Strich does bring up realism in this connection: in the military world that the actors evoke in their singing, the realistic worldview is made known. This is a worldview in which Wallenstein's belief in astrology, a belief that becomes his fate, finds its highest expression. Strich does not seem to have a good theoretical anchoring for the terms *realism* or *realistic*. The astrological aspects — denoted by the word Schiller first used, "*Fratze*" [caricatures] — are mentioned as a part of this nebulous notion of realism.

The inappropriateness of Wallenstein as a tragic character is mentioned as well; Schiller had to compensate for the attributes taken away from the historical Wallenstein (his rawness and monstrosity) by making him the incarnation of realism (Strich's word), a character who only values and calculates things in relation to his purposes. Here, at last, one can sense what Strich means by *realism* — it seems to have to do with Schiller's antithesis between the Ideal and the Real. This realist finds himself in thrall to natural necessity, while the idealist acknowledges only the necessity of reason.

Strich relates this realism directly to astrology in claiming that it becomes a sublime worldview that uses the stars as its symbolic form.

Max and Thekla (whose unhistoricity is not mentioned) represent the nobler world in which there is no goal and no use; here judgment is pronounced on Wallenstein not by a moralizing poet but within the drama itself. Strich sees this play darkly; the world of ideas has collapsed, and the world of realism does the same. This version of realism is cruel; it paints a picture of terrible truth without embellishment or idealization. What seems to be human happiness is, in reality, Wallenstein's temptation and his fate. The totality of life triumphs over the arrogance of individual will.

After finishing *Wallenstein,* says Strich, Schiller wrestled with the topic for his next play. He claimed to be tired of soldiers and heroes but, nevertheless, returned to historical sources for inspiration. Strich notes that after writing *Wallenstein,* Schiller felt that he could "master" historical material; here returns the notion of historical information as a substance to be molded and conquered. As Strich turns to *Maria Stuart,* he follows his post-Rankean predecessors by going initially to the historical sources Schiller used. He mentions the historical inaccuracies without criticizing them, although he uses the word that has negative connotations — "*Abweichungen*" — and judges them warranted by aesthetic and dramatic necessity. For example, the meeting of the two queens was structurally necessary so that the play would not fall apart into two unrelated halves; Mortimer symbolizes the temptations of life, so that the main character feels a tension between physical freedom and incarceration; Leicester's fictitious love creates tension over the issue of whether or not Maria will be rescued; and the confession and absolution make Maria's character development visible. Strich says that a historical drama should represent the "Geist der Geschichte" [spirit of history] (381): the conflicts between Reformation and Counter-Reformation, the state and the individual personality are brought to life in the figures of the two queens.

Turning to *Die Jungfrau von Orleans,* Strich follows the same pattern of first consulting Schiller's historical sources. He reminds the reader that Schiller found the source material for this play while he was working on *Maria Stuart.* After listing the sources he explains how history was necessary to Schiller's purpose (*history* in what sense is not clear; perhaps Strich means historical material?) — not for an accurate portrayal of Joan of Arc but for representing the Middle Ages. In the historical material, as one sees in his historical essays, Schiller had witnessed the miraculous power of idealism and needed no romantic (i.e. fictional) impulse to portray it. Strich claims that "*Geschichtswissenschaft*" — that is, scientific history — had proven that Schiller's version of the mysterious Joan of Arc was actually more historical than the picture to which his contemporaries had access, partly because he rescued her from the Voltairean ridicule that was fashionable at the time. He treated her with more honor and respect than Shakespeare did in *Henry VI*. The end of Schiller's play, Strich says, is rather freely drawn. After relating Johanna's death at the stake, Strich gives the "real" story; but he says that Schiller could not use such an ending, because his heroine had to die a beautiful death, reconciled to herself and to her people (a comment that is heard again and again). The dramatic plan is thus, once again, brought in to justify a change in the historical material. Strich concludes by making a statement about the two nations involved, one with political ties to Strich's contemporary situation: in the rhythm of the battle between France and England, a parallel rhythm of their inner experience unfolds. This fight is a world-historical symbol of the eternally fought battle between nature and the ideal.

Throughout his analysis Strich places more emphasis on rhetoric than on content. It is difficult to apprehend any structure to his argument. He seems to have assembled, pastichelike, comments already made about Schiller's historical plays in other sources. He waffles between opinions and then simply states that Schiller is the greatest German playwright of all time.

After the First World War, conditions in the new Weimar Republic generated a reevaluation of Schiller. The war provided a final blow to optimism about human achievement and confirmed the doubts expressed thirty years earlier by Nietzsche and others. How would Schiller's history-based dramas fare in this climate? One might hypothesize that they would be seen as hopelessly naive, out of date, rigidified. As we have seen, the use of Schiller in the classroom did as little to further voluntary reading or viewing as did Nietzsche's famous slur "Moraltrompeter von Säckingen" [moral trumpeter from Säckingen]. Art and culture in the Weimar Republic became characterized quite rapidly as avant-garde; how could a Schiller find any place there?

In addition, the privileged status of the literary critic as pedagogue, political interpreter or arbiter of taste had been in decline for nearly fifty years. Naturalist literary "criticism" had already expressed a fundamental hostility to critics; leftists believed that bourgeois critics had no objectivity because they were beholden to a capitalistic press. The role of critic fell increasingly to scholars at universities, who could, even more than their counterparts employed by journals, be accused of writing in isolation.

On the other hand, Schiller may have provided a refuge, a haven for the nostalgic; this theory can explain the surprising rebirth of interest in Schiller in the 1920s, and one that had none of the dire overtones of a Spengler. The critics who write about Schiller in this period sound so familiar. Hermann August Korff, writing in 1927, is most excited about his ideals and about how the early plays reflect an enthusiasm for the morally right and the later plays reflect a more sophisticated and cynical, though not less idealistic, view of world history. Throughout, according to Korff, Schiller is preoccupied with human greatness — something not particularly visible on the German literary agenda in 1927 — and how human greatness intersects with moral issues. Korff differentiates between Schiller's "Schauspiel" [drama], in which the "Weltgericht" [world court] plays out its trials, and Schiller's tragedies, embedded in the "Schauspiel," in which the hero (who always embodies human greatness) grapples both with the forces unleashed by society and with those within his/her own psyche.

After discussing how Schiller's philosophical writings are borne out in his plays, Korff turns to a discussion of *Wallenstein*. Like late nineteenth-century critics he mentions the issue of historical uncertainty in the motivations for Wallenstein's treason, which Schiller brought up in *Geschichte des dreßigjährigen Kriegs*. He continues with a discussion of Wallenstein's greatness; here, however, it is not clear if he is speaking of the historical general or Schiller's character. Eventually Korff makes a judgment: Wallenstein is a Napoleon in that both men were limitlessly ambitious because they exemplified "Gewissenlosigkeit" [lack of conscience]. He differentiates between outer limitlessness (greed, hunger for power, ambition) and inner limitlessness (lack of conscience) and claims that the latter is more dangerous, because a person with this trait will glorify any means to achieve a great end. (Of course, reading this text today forces one to think immediately of Hitler.)

At the same time, Korff moderates his judgment by bringing up Schiller's tactic for giving Wallenstein a more idealistic patina: his general is considering treason for the purpose of bringing peace to Europe.

Korff addresses the issue of fate by referring to the Prologue, in which Schiller gives fate only half the credit for Wallenstein's fall. It is not his fate, says Korff, but rather the way he handles it that not creates only the tragedy but also ennobles Wallenstein. This pattern is the heart of Schiller's tragedies: a hero rises, falls, and shows a certain dignity in his/her fall. The same thing happens in *Maria Stuart* and, to a certain extent, in *Die Jungfrau von Orleans*. He claims that it is incorrect to call Schiller's last plays tragedies of fate: fate plays a role, but it is not that which is most important; it is how the hero goes to meet that fate – in which he or she has surely had a hand, if in an unexpected way.

The astrological aspects of the play are mentioned not as unhistorical or deleterious to the tragic effect — though Korff does express sympathy for Otto Ludwig's disgust at this element – but, rather, as evidence that the formerly great Wallenstein is great no more. The fact that he lends credence during such a fateful hour to signs that are so illusory can be attributed to his "losgelöster Verstand" [loosened powers of reason]. Schiller gives us initially a picture of Wallenstein's greatness to which the figure onstage does not measure up, and the belief in astrology confirms his weakness. His greatness at the end is thereby made that much more palpable. Otto Ludwig was incorrect in calling Wallenstein "pathological"; "temporarily weak" would have been a better formulation.

The greater tragedy that Korff brings up is the tragedy of the unmoral world of politics, which can just as easily be called the tragedy of realism. He does not see Max as a hopelessly idealistic fool but as a morally laudable hero who shows the higher-road alternative to Wallenstein. The general is, however, incapable of following that road because of his lack of ideals. He can mourn Max's death; he can feel this loss intensely; but he can act only heroically, not morally.

Before leaving *Wallenstein* Korff draws historical parallels, putting Schiller into the place of seer. For Korff, however, the parallels are painfully close. He sees the dilemma facing Wallenstein to be the same one facing Germany before the First World War. Germany grew to greatness, and her enemies began to feel threatened at the saber-rattling and drew together to protect themselves against her. The atmosphere of mutual distrust brewed tensions to a point where the mobilization of Russia forced Germany's hand; the violation of Belgian neutrality completed the act merely thought of up until then. Korff alters an aphorism from the time: Germany was not Hamlet, but Wallenstein.

In his final words on *Wallenstein* Korff considers Schiller's aphorism about the world court and says that "wenn die Weltgeschichte wirklich das Weltgericht ist, dann ist sie tragischerweise ein Gericht, in dem das Gute und das Böse gleichermaßen, wenn auch aus verschiedenen Gründen, untergeht" [if world history is truly the world court, then it is tragically a court in which both good and evil, although for different reasons, are annihilated] (262).

Korff spends little time on either *Maria Stuart* or *Die Jungfrau von Orleans*. He prefaces his remarks by noting that since Schiller is taught in the schools, some may assume that it is easy to read him. He speaks about the different levels on which one can do so, then concentrates on the historical level. Schiller's later plays are historical inasmuch as the playwright has taken historical materials and used them for his purposes. Korff justifies this practice in a novel way: history is the storage space for "alles Großen" [everything great]. Schiller takes pictures not from the past but from eternity. Rather than being a colorful collection of potential dramatic materials, Korff claims, history for Schiller was an assemblage of material in which the humanly significant is preserved as it is in myth and legend. The relationship that obtained between the ancients and myth is the same that exists between moderns and history: history is a showcase of the great symbols of humanity. It is the poet's duty to go about his work as a sculptor does, chiseling out that which is significant from the mass of history. In this part of his essay Korff casts history into an entirely different light, suspending the scientificity of history. His argument legitimizes Schiller's discarding of events or dates or even personages that do not fit "true" history on grounds that have nothing to do with poetic license but with the nature of history itself. In fact, the argument goes further than legitimization — it congratulates Schiller on his method. Korff is claiming that the genre of historical drama is more historical than any other critic has allowed.

In his brief glance at *Maria Stuart* Korff brings up the meeting of the queens as an example of the climax displaying the entire main thrust of a drama. Maria acts decisively in sacrificing her life to maintain her human dignity. But there is a purpose for Schiller beyond giving an example of heroic behavior, for, as Korff notes, the moral world order almost always makes use of human passions to assist justice. In an even briefer glance at *Die Jungfrau von Orleans* Korff aligns himself with critics who see Johanna as an incarnation of a patriotic ideal and brings up the same antithesis on which he focused in more detail in his discussion of *Wallenstein:* the fate of all that is good and noble when it comes into contact with reality. He does not bring up historical particulars in either discussion; perhaps he believed that he had addressed the issue in adequate detail in the *Wallenstein* commentary.

Hans Heinrich Borcherdt (1887–1964), writing in 1929, begins his argument as any critic from the late nineteenth century would by pointing first to Schiller's historical studies and their relationship to his historical dramas. But Borcherdt unexpectedly defends Schiller's historical essays, which by this time had been thoroughly discredited and ridiculed: through these writings, he says, Schiller wished to stimulate the mind and the moral sense. Borcherdt's defense rests on the grounds that Schiller's interest was not historical facts but the meaning behind historical development; for this reason it is meaningless to attack his historical work from a professional standpoint. The philosophical value of these writings remains for Borcherdt even as the details are wanting, because freedom of the mind and the interplay of coincidence and will, of reason and effect, comprise the meaning of history.

Borcherdt views Schiller's Wallenstein as a realist (and here we understand *realist* to mean "political pragmatist"); the dramatist needed to provide an idealistic counterpart, and for this reason Schiller created Max Piccolomini. Even this realist Wallenstein is not historical, however, but universal. Borcherdt claims that Schiller wished to juxtapose the eternally realistic with the eternally idealistic; since in this instance the historical materials did not provide the idealist, however, Schiller needed to create him. Borcherdt maintains that the general, eternal aspects of the play retain their importance; when these aspects are not visible, even the historical aspects lose their importance. It is possible that Spengler's dark views of the lack of vitality of Western society are making themselves felt here. The flight to a world where ideal types interact is far less painful than the view of sterile individual historical figures; *Wallenstein* is a play that lends itself quite well to such an interpretation.

As Borcherdt turns to *Maria Stuart* (*Die Jungfrau von Orleans* is not discussed in terms of its historical background), however, he notes Schiller's dramatic purpose — to make the material tragic — and begins to cast aspersions on Schiller's historical tinkering. He lists the many "Abweichungen von der Historie," including the age of the women, the time of Maria's imprisonment, Leicester's love for Maria, the character Mortimer, Maria's confession and communion, and, above all, the meeting of the two queens, which Schiller himself admits is "unwahrscheinlich" [a German word meaning "improbable" but containing the words *truth* and *seem*). But he had to do it to provide Sophoclean irony: what Maria most wants turns into her curse. On the other hand, claims Borcherdt, Schiller uses many accurate facts from the past without any dramatic purpose whatsoever, facts that give the impression of a historical drama. There is a split, in other words: the historical material is simply a poetic mantle, and the substance of the play, as well as the characterizations, are completely unhistorical. The fictitious character Mortimer, claims Borcherdt, is, nevertheless, rationalized because Schiller needed to personify the allurements of life in a single character. This strategy runs parallel to the way Schiller incarnates the different roads of political practice in the various statesmen — Burleigh, Leicester, and Davidson — to bring them together in the figure of Elizabeth herself. Similarly, the characters surrounding Maria embody the powers that are active within their queen. This is why Schiller found the meeting of the queens an unconditional necessity, for the opposites unite themselves in both figures. This fictional scene in which the queens meet is not only the ideal but also the dramatic centerpiece of the play, the point to which all that precedes it leads and from which everything else issues. It is this aspect that makes the drama Schiller's most structurally compact and most cameo-like. Borcherdt thus seems to return to his prioritizing of universal types (Mortimer as embodiment of the temptations of life) and to reshaping historical materials for dramatic purposes.

The critics of the 1920s, then, seem to be unaffected for the most part by Spengler's pessimism; their split approach to Schiller's plays seems, rather, to mirror the ideas of Karl Mannheim. While nodding to the "science" of history and taking into consideration the historical sources Schiller used (and sometimes resorting to a nineteenth-century scolding about "*Abweichungen*"), they seem to be able simultaneously to laud Schiller's ability to paint the broader sense of history onstage.

One year before Borcherdt's analysis of *Wallenstein* and *Maria Stuart*, Max Kommerell wrote a study titled *Der Dichter als Führer* (The Poet as Leader) that put forward the notion of an influential, strong poet; here Schiller takes his place with Goethe, Klopstock, and Herder, among others. It is right to look at the title and shudder; as Helmut Koopmann notes, the chapter on Schiller is a prime example of the dehistoricization and shifting of emphasis that prepared a heroicized and militarized picture of Schiller long before National Socialism. Koopmann (776) connects this demonized Schiller with the monograph that can surely claim the most ominous title, Hans Fabricius's *Schiller als Kampfgenosse Hitlers* (Schiller as Hitler's Comrade in Battle, 1934). As we turn to Schiller's co-optation during the darkest years of German history, it is with an awareness that complex forces gave rise to the popularity of National Socialism; not least among them was the attempt to reestablish a credible order after a time of ferocious disorientation. It was also as a reaction to the rationality of the nineteenth century, which had failed to produce better living conditions for the German people, that the irrationality of fascism gained hold.

Works Cited

Albert, Claudia. *Deutsche Klassiker im Nationalsozialismus: Schiller, Kleist, Hölderlin*. Stuttgart: Metzler, 1994, 48–50.

Berman, Russell A. "Literary Criticism from Empire to Dictatorship, 1870–1933," in *A History of German Literary Criticism, 1730–1980*, ed. Peter Uwe Hohendahl. Lincoln and London: U of Nebraska P, 1988, 277–357.

Borcherdt, Hans Heinrich. *Schiller: Seine Geistige und künstleriche Entwicklung*. Leipzig: Quelle & Meyer, 1929, 80–134.

Dilthey, Wilhelm. *Von deutscher Dichtung und Musik*. Leipzig and Berlin: Teubner, 1933, 325–427.

Gardiner, Patrick. *Theories of History*. New York: Free Press, 1959.

Grumley, John E. *History and Totality: Radical Historicism from Hegel to Foucault*. London and New York: Routledge, 1989.

Heller, Erich. *The Disinherited Mind: Essays in Modern German Literature and Thought*, third ed. New York: Barnes & Noble, 1971, 181–96.

Iggers, Georg G. *The German Conception of History: The National Tradition of Historical Thought from Herder to the Present.* Middletown CT: Wesleyan UP, 1983.

Kommerell, Max. *Der Dichter als Führer in der deutschen Klassik: Klopstock, Herder, Goethe, Schiller, Jean Paul, Hölderlin.* Berlin: Bondi, 1928, 177–303.

Koopmann, Helmut, ed. *Schiller-Handbuch.* Stuttgart: Körner, 1998, 776.

Korff, Hermann August. *Geist der Goethezeit: Versuch einer ideellen Entwicklung der klassisch-romantischen Literaturgeschichte,* vol. 2: *Klassik. Erstes Buch: Weltanschauung.* Leipzig: J. J. Weber, 1927.

Ludwig, Albert. *Das Urteil über Schiller im neunzehnten Jahrhundert: Eine Revision seines Prozesses.* Bonn: Friedrich Cohen, 1905.

Mannheim, Karl. *Essays on the Sociology of Knowledge,* ed. Paul Kecskemeti. New York: Oxford UP, 1952, 84–133.

Oellers, Norbert, ed. *Schiller — Zeitgenosse aller Epochen. Dokumente zur Wirkungsgeschichte Schillers in Deutschland,* vol. 2: 1860–1966. Munich: Beck, 1976, 1–14.

Strich, Fritz. Schiller: *Sein Leben und sein Werk,* in *Schillers Sämtliche Werke,* vol. 13. Berlin: Deutsche Buch-Gemeinschaft, 1912, 340–65, 376–400.

Wellek, René. *A History of Modern Criticism: 1750–1950: The Later Nineteenth Century.* New Haven and London: Yale UP, 1965, 320–56.

4: Schiller's Late Historical Plays and the Third Reich

TWO AUTHORITARIAN REGIMES in twentieth-century Germany adopted ideological stances that dictated how history and historiography were to be interpreted or manipulated. Adolf Hitler's National Socialism came to official power in January 1933, and Stalinist Communism was established in the German Democratic Republic in October 1949. In both cases the ruling forces found it necessary to co-opt the representation of history to the service of ideology, and the prevalent concept of history returned to a teleological form, reminiscent of, though not identical to, Schlözer's concept of *Universalgeschichte*. Historical narrative needed to be aligned under or created toward an ideology that traced a trajectory with an endpoint in, respectively, the triumph of the Aryan master race and the establishment of a workers' state. Fascism and Marxism occupy opposite ends of the political spectrum, but their similarities are well summarized by Ernst Nolte: "Fascism is antimarxism which seeks to destroy the enemy by the evolution of a radically opposed and yet related ideology and by the use of almost identical and yet typically modified methods" (20–21). (While Nolte has fallen into disrepute for controversial theories about the Holocaust, his *The Three Faces of Fascism* is still held in considerable regard.) Nolte's comments also allude to the essential negativism of National Socialism, a negativism that makes the elaboration of an ideology and a poetics to accompany it problematic.

While the above-stated difficulties make it challenging to generalize about the "Third Reich" criticism of Schiller's later historical plays, some central theories can be proposed. The characters are seen as "historical" inasmuch as they are representations of some past reality. They receive more credit, however, for being representative of humankind in general, thus satisfying the National Socialist demand for "*völkisch*"-ness. [The Nazi term *völkisch* is impossible to translate into English in a way that will render the scope of its surface innocuousness, its deeper malignancy, and its ultimate lack of precision, but an approximation would be "folkishness."] Characters striving for greater moral freedom (and especially those doing so at great personal risk, as in the case of Schiller's *Die Jungfrau von Orleans*) were particularly appreciated as an example for all Germans.

The Hitler regime controlled the distribution and substance of written documents through the government and through the NSDAP (National Sozialistische Deutsche Arbeiterpartei [National Socialist German Workers' Party, or Nazi Party]). In the case of the former, a dense hierarchy of agencies under the Abteilung VIII im Reichsministerium für Volksaufklärung und Propaganda [Section VIII in the Reich Ministry of People's Enlightenment and Propaganda], headed by Joseph Goebbels, controlled literature, art, music, film, theater, and the press. The Kuratorium für das deutsche Fachschrifttum [Board of Control of German Professional Writing] oversaw literary criticism, and the Reichskulturkammer [Reich Council on Culture] controlled the eventually scarce supply of paper. The interpretation of literary texts was to be aimed, officially, at the "enlightenment of the people and propaganda." On the party side Alfred Rosenberg, Beauftragter des Führers für die Überwachung der gesamten geistigen und weltanschaulichen Schulung und Erziehung der NSDAP [The Führer's Commissioner for the Control of the Entire Intellectual and Worldview Schooling and Education of the NSDAP], provided a counterweight to Goebbels's provenance, resulting in a competition that probably allowed for more freedom of expression than existed under the later GDR regime. The duties of these agencies were to control new literary production as tightly as possible and to promote and organize the selection and reevaluation of older texts. In order for the tasks that would normally fall to a literary critic to be performed, aesthetic standards acceptable to National Socialism had to be established (Ruppelt, 5).

The difficulties of establishing such an aesthetics were considerable. As stated above, National Socialism was more easily described in terms of what it was not than what it was. As Ruppelt says, "National-Socialist ideology strikes us in its variations as a muddle of ideas and conceptions that can be organized around certain main points but that hardly lend themselves to systematization" (6). To examine the history of a collective rather than of individuals (monarchs, popes, etc.), the unifying factor within the group needs to be defined. For the National Socialists, the common factor was a mixture of blood, race, and "*Volk*," and the basis for this definition lay in nineteenth-century race theories propounded by Joseph Artur de Gobineau, Houston Stewart Chamberlain, and others. These theories, Charles Darwin's studies of natural selection, and Herder's and Jacob Grimm's notions of epochal specificity and nationhood combined to produce a "theory" of history quite different from Ranke's scientific, "wie es eigentlich geschehen" model. History is here defined as a struggle "der naturgegebenen Völker und Rassen" [of the naturally determined peoples and races] (Werner, 9), a winnowing process that could result in ultimate racial degradation but, if vigorously counteracted, would end in the victory of the Aryan race. Among the focal points Ruppelt mentions, in addition to blood and race, are "*völkisch*"-ness, the presence of a strong leader, emphasis on feeling and irrationality rather than on logic and reason, valuing of militarism and heroism, the superiority of the country over the city, and the precedence of the nation, *das Reich,* over the individual. The ideas of "nation" and "*Volk*" became enmeshed in the Nazi state and created tension. Because of the emphasis on "*Volk*," history needed to focus on the collective; on the other hand, the cult of the hero or *Führer* demanded attention to the individual and his (nearly always *his*) bloodlines. While the concept of "*Volk*" proved too vague to measure quantitatively, the issue of "*Blut*" [blood] and all that accompanied it — height, hair color, skull measurements — seemed to satisfy the demand for scientificity.

The bifurcation of the scientific view of "*Blut*" and the emotional attachment to "*Volk*" is reflected in the split view of the German/Germanic past. History became, above all, the study of how the "Germanic" peoples from ancient times through the Middle Ages wandered, conquered, and civilized, and how the Western European influences that culminated in the Renaissance and the Enlightenment wielded a negative influence on the truly German spirit of the Reformation and Goethean idealism. In other words, "history" was used selectively in a perversion of Herder's notion of the "Eigenwertigkeit einzelner geschichtlichen Epochen" [individual value of single historical epochs] (Gilman, xiii); dates and places were used energetically as support for the notion of the supremacy of Germanic tribes during the Middle Ages.

But by 1933 "history" hardly meant history any longer. It was a curious mixture of anthropology, mythology (the Old Norse sagas, in particular, became popular reading), ideology, and anxiety. History became future-focused rather than retrospective, tightly allied with the notion of fate, and the accuracy of representation of the past became subservient to the propagandistic aspects of establishing the history of German "*Blut und Boden*" [blood and soil] as a basis and justification for future world domination. Those who did wish to pay attention to historical details were treated condescendingly: "Interest in historical 'particulars' was naturally highly unusual — their study could be safely left to scholars oblivious to the world, [while we remain] conscious of the fact that because of lack of racial schooling they did not understand the greater connections" (Werner, 37–38). Hermann Wanderscheck's words demonstrate how well the National Socialists fooled themselves: "Limitless desecration of historical truth against the spirit of the nation was characteristic for a time that saw in the dramatic form a repository for political incitement" (quoted in Gilman, 109).

Much ink was spent on trying to establish a National Socialist aesthetics, but this "poetics" remained conceptually weak, reliant on a discourse rife with such prefixes as "*art-*," "*volks-*" and "*boden-*." This weakness is not surprising in an era that prided itself on the need for propaganda (which appealed more to emotions and irrationality than to logic and reason) to achieve political aims that would supposedly benefit the German people. The combination of desires — to support theories of genetic superiority scientifically, to appeal to the emotions through propaganda, to rely on historical evidence to highlight the age-old glory of the Germanic people, and to disregard historical evidence that would prove otherwise — resulted in an anxiety that permeates nearly all scholarship carried out during the Hitler regime. Schiller criticism is no exception.

The function of the critic, as can be seen, was in some ways an echo of what Schiller had wanted nearly 150 years earlier: to select and promote worthy art that would help educate the people. It was easy to decide which texts and writers were not desirable under the negative conditions of National Socialism; it was more difficult to find positive models. Schiller became useful not only because he provided self-sacrificing heroes but also because he was recast, *Die Horen* notwithstanding, as a "*völkisch*" writer. His status as a classic within German letters made him good compensation for the writers who, because of Jewish heritage, Marxist leanings, or other undesirable traits, had to be removed from the canon. National Socialist scholars pounced on Schiller and energetically set out to "rehabilitate" him after years of neglect during the "decadent" Weimar Republic. It was only under National Socialism that Schiller could finally and truly be appreciated. GDR scholars would use the same approach to "reform" Schiller beginning in 1946.

In contrast to the more homogeneous publications of the scholarly community in the GDR, literary scholars during the Nazi period, at least until 1939, were given relative freedom in interpreting Schiller. To be sure, there was no room in Hitler's Third Reich for Marxist interpretations. But within the range of non-Marxist interpretational possibilities, as Sander Gilman points out, scholars had more intellectual freedom than one would expect. Nevertheless, scholars tended to adhere to Nazi ideology or, at least, to mouth its rhetoric. Gilman gives three reasons for this conformity: "*Berufsopportunismus*" [professional opportunism], the belief that promotions and other favors would fall to those more clearly in line with party ideology; the feeling among Germanists that their field of endeavor was finally raised to the status of a kind of "*Gralswissenschaft*" [grail science, a term that connotes succinctly the exaggerated reverence accorded to all things German]; and, most ominous, the confirmation of already-held beliefs in Nazi ideology and the possibility for their further development (ix-xii). None of the critics of this period appears to be immune to Nazi ideology, and some, indeed, embrace it. Two of them, however — Gerhard Fricke and Benno von Wiese — seem to pay less attention to it than their colleagues, focusing on the text rather than on the context. Whether this stance qualified them as internal emigrants is a topic outside the scope of this study.

Theater was an important tool during the Third Reich. It appealed to a collective (the audience) far more than to an individual reader, promoting a feeling of belonging to "*das Volk*." Basing their argument on Schiller's essay *Die Schaubühne als moralische Anstalt betrachtet*, National Socialists contended that their attitude toward the theater was in line with Schiller's, inasmuch as he, as well as they, saw it as an "Erziehungsmittel für das ganze Volk" [tool for education for the whole people] (Haider-Pregler, 207). The important function of historical drama, in particular, is discussed by Wanderscheck in 1939. He points to the renewed need for the political drama, because, in its representation of the "militant" (an important word) struggle for the spirit and soul of the German man and his "*volkhafte*" [racial] mission, it has entered into a new relationship with history. He urges dramatists to pay special attention to this mission in their writing and to take as their goal the dramatization of historical and political events. The purpose of poetry becomes politicized, once again, as Wanderscheck claims that the poet must become engrossed in living, "*volkbestimmenden*" [people-determining] history and must become a prophet and seer in showing the way for the people to go. He ends this argument by claiming that "the element of history has reclaimed for the drama that totality that is embodied in the authoritarian leadership of the national-socialist state" (quoted in Gilman, 110). The haziness of this rhetoric belies the ominous message underneath. Goebbels, too, had a new mission in mind for historical drama: the dramatist was to show the greatness of the historical process and to ensure that the artistic form achieved the same greatness on an aesthetic level. While both Wanderscheck and Goebbels are primarily interested in exhorting new or current writers, it is plausible that critics looking at Schiller would have such guidelines in mind as they reevaluated his late historical plays. They certainly played a role in the revival of the plays onstage.

Schiller's later historical plays do not lend themselves to interpretations along the lines of genetic makeup. His characters tend not to be Germanic types; Schiller himself was described as having less than optimal blood lines by National Socialist standards ("*dinarisch*" [Dinarian] mixed with the more desirable "*nordisch*" [Nordic]). Although a more thorough look at the National Socialist view of Kant lies outside the scope of this study, it is worth mentioning that because Kant, according to Ludwig Klages's system, was seen as part of the "*graecojudaisch*" and "*logozentrisch*" tradition, he wielded a negative influence on Schiller. But as Werner Deubel notes, this harmful influence was "fortunately" counteracted and tempered by his friendship with the more "graecogermanisch" and "biozentrisch" Goethe (Ruppelt, 61–63). Schiller critics during the period of National Socialism tended to focus, instead, on issues related to the "*völkisch*"-ness of Schiller's plays, as well as on the idea of "*Führertum*" [leadership]. For these reasons it is easy to see why *Wallenstein* is the favorite play of National Socialists, followed closely by *Die Jungfrau von Orleans*. The medieval historical connections of the latter, through the crucial part that Burgundy (a questionably German piece of land) plays politically in Schiller's drama, make it even more tantalizing. *Maria Stuart*, on the other hand, is less favored, partly because it showcases French classicism and, thus, the negative influence "Western Europe" was thought to have wielded over German-speaking lands; in addition, National Socialist ideology had little sympathy for politically powerful women or for the English in general.

Because of the particular perspective created by what passes as "Nazi poetics," problems emerge in analyzing much of the "Third Reich" Schiller criticism in terms of how history is perceived and portrayed. In the first place, it is often unclear whether the critic is referring to Schiller's character or to the historical personage (and, in some cases, it is even questionable whether the reference might not be to *Schiller's* historical personage as portrayed in his historical writings). It is often not even mentioned that Schiller created some of the characters himself (Max Piccolomini, Mortimer), and the functions of these characters are consequently not highlighted in terms of Schiller's purpose. The notion of Schiller as a revolutionary occurs here, as well as in GDR scholarship; his support of the idea of revolution and his ambivalence about the bloody results of the French Revolution were highlighted as grounds for identifying him as a would-be supporter of the bloodless *Machtergreifung* [seizure of power]. But outside of this particular historical issue, history plays a multivalent role within Schiller criticism. It is often difficult to ascertain whether the critic means "history" or "fate," for these notions are intertwined within National Socialist ideology.

Another difficulty is presented by the National Socialist prose itself. In a poetics that values emotion over reason, academic prose becomes less dependent on logical discourse and more prone to emotional language consisting of bursts of rhetoric not always directed toward a line of reasoning. Some critics are careful to use the proper vocabulary but less concerned about providing a cogent argument. The work of the Germanist Herbert Cysarz (1896–1985) falls most definitely under the category of "ideologically colored" scholarship, and it displays the difficulties mentioned. His 1934 work on Schiller shows all the passion and attention to feeling (often at the expense of cogency) that one would expect from criticism of this period. (Indeed, some critics thought that he was a throwback to expressionism.) His treatment of history is personified: he speaks, for example, of Wallenstein wishing to grasp the throat of history, to trample its neck. Where it is not personified, it merges with the concept of fate. Occasionally, Cysarz refers to "actual" history as Schiller read it in his sources (especially in the discussion of *Maria Stuart,* where Cysarz lists all the standard "inaccuracies" from the meeting of the queens to the difference in their ages). In each of the three plays, history assumes a different role. In *Wallenstein* it is a substance that the general wishes to control (and it is here, especially, that it becomes confused with "fate"); in *Maria Stuart* it becomes an irritating detail that Schiller quite rightly "straightens": "Um des Prozesses willen hat Schiller Vieles ausgibig zurechtgebogen" [For the sake of the trial, Schiller bent much back into shape] (340). In *Die Jungfrau von Orleans* the condescension toward history reaches its peak: Cysarz sees the play as a philosophico-religious tour de force that has shaken the dust of history off its feet so well that history is barely mentioned in the discussion of the work.

Werner Deubel's scholarship also features rhetorical flourishes and hazy concepts, while concentrating on Schiller in light of a "scientific" system: Klages's categories of "*logozentrisch*" as opposed to "*biozentrisch*" orientation. Little mention is made of history except in one notable instance: Deubel discusses *Maria Stuart* and *Die Jungfrau von Orleans* in fairly disparaging terms, claiming that their effect can be explained by a seer's necromantic eye for history's pictorial qualities. He decries the dramas for their overabundance of grandiose historical scenes, which fool the viewer into ignoring the paleness of the soulful aspects and the flatness of the tragic qualities of the characters. This technique, Deubel warns, creates a situation where the viewer can easily be deceived into mistaking Schiller's creation for true history. Deubel thus refers to necromancy, the attempt to communicate with the dead in order to obtain information about the future or to influence its course, in the same breath in which he mentions "the science of history." For Deubel history is both magic and science, and Schiller's use of it casts a spell on an audience that is more real than "true" history. It is obvious that Deubel could not congratulate Schiller on his potential as a propagandist.

In his article written in honor of Schiller's 175th birthday (1934) Walter Linden, from 1926 to 1934 head of the "scientific" department of the *Zeitschrift für Deutschkunde,* lauds *Wallenstein* as the playwright's most perfect historical drama, partly because he was able to tame (Linden uses the word *bewältigen* [conquer]) history. At the same time, he claims that Schiller put history on the stage "in lebensvoller Objektivität" [objectively] (523). These statements are typical of National Socialist scholarship not only in their appreciation for *Wallenstein* but also in their reference to German people and "their" literature. In line with this orientation Linden claims a certain patriotism for Schiller, averring that *Wallenstein* was not written for humanity but specifically for the German people and their particular issues. He bases his argument on the fact that Wallenstein wishes to establish a German peace, one that will put an end to the destruction of German-speaking lands. Linden compares Max Piccolomini to Wallenstein: both face conflicting forces, and Wallenstein falls because he chooses treason; Max, on the other hand, dies a hero's death together with his forces, his "*Volk*." Many National Socialist scholars point to the difference between these deaths in terms of heroism (Wallenstein killed in his sleep, Max on the battlefield); few, however, point out the issue of Max's unhistoricity.

Maria Stuart is virtually ignored by Linden, and as he moves on to *Die Jungfrau von Orleans* he reiterates the issue he sees at the heart of *Wallenstein:* the "general" human point of view. By this phrase Linden means the close relationship of the (true) hero to his people. Max dies with his "*Volk*," as does Johanna. Even Johanna's guilt is tied to her humanity, her falling in love, and makes her more "*völkisch*." Linden concludes by pointing out Schiller's importance as a political dramatist, claiming not only that he established that genre for the Germans but also that he allowed a truly political and history-creating power to flow through this particular drama by filling it with personal sacrifice, willingness to contribute (one's own life), hardness, determination in the face of fate, conscious choice of self-destruction, and heroic, dignified death. While one can recognize here a tendency to National Socialist rhetoric, especially in the last phrase, the word "*geschichteschaffende*" [history-creating], catches one's eye. Once again the notion of history is vague but obviously allied with fate; it is also something that can be created rather than merely recorded.

Julius Petersen, an academic who spent several of the early years of the century at educational institutions outside Germany (including Yale University), wrote two Schiller studies that will be examined here. In the earlier piece, published in 1934, Petersen points to the intimate relationship between the hero and his/her people, especially in *Wallenstein* and *Die Jungfrau von Orleans*, and the responsibility the hero owes to those around him/her. Petersen is one of the few National Socialist critics who treat the question of historical accuracy directly, although he avoids its practical application in critiquing Schiller's plays. For example, pointing out that newer interpretations of the Wallenstein material prove that the general wanted to free Germany of all invaders, Swedish as well as Spanish, and to reestablish its unity, he notes that Schiller alludes to this interpretation but does not emphasize it. *Maria Stuart* is labeled a drama of historical authenticity without a mention of the unhistorical meeting of the queens. Petersen views as "historical" the compression of the two sides of the religious question in the figures of the Protestant Burleigh and the Catholic Mortimer. There is no mention of historical accuracy in *Die Jungfrau von Orleans*. Objective truth obviously takes a back seat to propaganda; Schiller's plays are considered in the light of the moral lessons they can provide, not in regard to their presentation of history on stage. A historical example is, however, cited to support Schiller's method and, subsequently, National Socialist ideology. The old German view of leader and followers is reflected in Wallenstein, claims Petersen, and the old themes of the folk and heroic epics emerge from the depth of the "Siegfried nature" of his young men — in particular, Max Piccolomini, whose choice between honor and loyalty Petersen compares to the choice made by Margrave Rüdiger in the *Nibelungenlied*. (Petersen seems to have forgotten that Max was actually Italian.) This reflection of ancient German ways, however, came out of Schiller without his knowing of it, as an unconscious cultural inheritance. Here the tendency can be seen — one common not only to the National Socialist critics — to blend Schiller's life, theory, and works into one homogeneous flow. Lily Hohenstein will also take this tack.

Petersen begins his 1940 monograph by pointing to the confusion reigning over the designation "historical drama." It should, he avers, provide a bridge "zwischen dem *zeitlosen* und dem *gleichzeitigen*" [between the timeless and the simultaneous] (2). Distinguishing between "epic" and "balladlike" historical drama, he claims that Shakespeare's histories fall into the former category and Schiller's *Wallenstein* into the latter: while Shakespeare brings the time more sharply into focus, Schiller emphasizes the space and provides an opportunity for pregnant moments and connections to be shown on stage so that the whole panorama of history becomes visible, if only in segments (2). He points to the tension between the presence of the theatrical moment and the past-flavored historical material but also to the need to transcend that tension in order to draw connections between the past and the present (propounding, once again, the moral value of theater). In this way, history is relieved of its "*Einmaligkeit*" [singularity], its quality of having occurred but once, and given a more universal meaning as the historical approaches the mythical.

Petersen is the only National Socialist critic considered in this study who attempts an analysis of how history works within the framework of historical drama. Before addressing this issue, he applies himself to the question of historical accuracy. He does possess certain standards, particularly in the areas of simultaneity and chronology. He frowns at the way Schiller's Wallenstein negotiates with Gustav Adolf, who was actually no longer alive at the time, calling this juggling of time "nicht tragbar" [not supportable] (7). He never sets clear boundaries for what is "*tragbar*," however; in discussing *Maria Stuart*, for example, he does not mention the meeting of the queens or their altered ages or tell why these inaccuracies are acceptable but a meeting between Wallenstein and Gustav Adolf is not. He attempts to set boundaries for the "supportable" at least schematically by laying down a general principle: the closer the dramatist can keep to the course of history, the less the credibility of the action needs to justify itself. Mortimer is mentioned as a fictitious character, but Schiller's motivation for creating him is not explored. Despite the attention he pays to the historical, Petersen denies that Schiller's dramas serve the function of "historical education" by subsuming the historical under the universal. For Petersen as (he claims) for Lessing, Goethe, and Schiller, poetry is more philosophical than history, and the final, lyrical paragraph of the study shows the emotional tone of critical discourse in the Third Reich as well as providing a commentary on Petersen's view of historical drama. He claims that dramatized history and dramatized myth are like two bodies of water in which the past mirrors itself. Dramatized history is a raging stream; myth is a lake that feeds the stream. Dramatized history comes back again and again to calmer bodies of water; dramatized myth seems calm on the surface but in subterranean (subaqueous?) ways draws new material from the colors and light of the wind and weather (56). Petersen thus cloaks the relationship in metaphor and mystery, and this treatment reflects the attitude of National Socialists to history: there is no essential difference between it and myth.

A prominent literary scholar who was an early and convinced Nazi, Gerhard Fricke made his mark as one of the main speakers at the book burning in Göttingen in May 1933. He left Germany for Turkey after the war; he returned to Germany in 1960 to work at the University of Cologne but was forced into retirement five years later because of his National Socialist past. He is one of the few Third Reich critics whose work is still considered of value, primarily because he focused less on the ideology of Nazism than on the texts themselves. His being given the editorship of the Hanser edition of Schiller's works shows the credit he received for his insight despite his political past.

Fricke argues for the autonomy of the author, which immediately sets him apart from other Third Reich critics. At the same time, he advocates the idea that literature is national, not universal, as do all National Socialist critics, so this autonomy is tempered by the mysterious power of the "*Volk*" and the ground in which it is rooted. In his 1943 study Fricke traces the superiority of the "Goethezeit" [time of Goethe] to what came between it and the Third Reich but also shows its weakness: too much emphasis on philosophical matters and not enough on material. German classicism also based itself on individuals and did not place enough emphasis on the earth; Herbert Smith, however, sees this comment as an attempt on Fricke's part to reduce the tension between his belief in the autonomy of the author, which would agree with the prioritizing of the individual, and Nazi ideology. Smith also points out that Fricke saw Schiller's interest in history as limited by what Schiller wished to extract from it: examples of individuals attaining freedom. As Fricke said, all of the seemingly historico-political dramas are actually dramas of inner, moral freedom. Schiller saw humans and their destinies either from above (from a philosophical stance) or from within, in the moral center of the individual (Smith, 27). While Fricke begins his monograph with a nod in the direction of National Socialism, he returns to his own text-based, deductive interpretation of the plays, interpretations that have more in common with Federal Republic studies than with those of his contemporaries in their lessened concern with the political or historical atmosphere surrounding the genesis of the texts.

A giant in Schiller scholarship who has, like Fricke, retained his authority and credibility to the present day is Benno von Wiese. Unlike Fricke, Wiese joined the Nazi party under duress and without conviction, according to his own account. One of the most prolific and widely respected of Germanists, Wiese also coedited volumes of the *Schiller Nationalausgabe*. He walks a double path similar to Fricke's, beginning his study *Die Dramen Schillers: Politik und Tragödie* (Schiller's Dramas: Politics and Tragedy) with the intent of reinterpreting Schiller's plays in the spirit of the new age. But Wiese works both sides of various critical issues, pointing to the contextual as well as the universal aspects of Schiller's work and finding value in how his texts work within the prevailing ideology as well as within the boundaries of the texts themselves. He refers to Schiller's view of history in his foreword, claiming that Schiller's historical studies were as important to the development of his theories about tragedy as was his engagement with Kant. Schiller kept wrestling with the essence of history, whose deeper meaning he found not "an den zeitgebundenen, aufgeklärten Humanitäts- und Fortschrittsidealen, sondern an dem tragischen, innerweltlichen Schicksalsgedanken aufgeht, der die Tragödie als Geschichte und die Geschichte als Tragödie versteht" [in the time-bound, enlightened ideals of humanity and progress, but rather in the tragic, inner-worldly notion of destiny, which understands tragedy as history, history as tragedy] (11–12). Wiese goes on to call the historical in Schiller's plays instances of living fields of power.

Erich Jäger's article on leadership and fellowship in *Wallenstein* says little about the historical until the end. Jäger speaks of Wallenstein and his men as two historical poles and refers to the tensions that run between them. In what way they are "historical" is not stated; he ends his article by pointing to a historical event mirrored in the play, the formation of a "*Volksgemeinschaft*" [people's association] between the people and their leader. Although this association did not succeed in Schiller's play, Jäger sees its potential for the future; unstated, of course, is that it is already occurring within the Third Reich.

Rudolf Giese is more intensely involved with the question of Schiller's relationship to history than are many of his colleagues. He cites the usual material pertinent to Schiller's view of history, particularly the famous definition from *Über das Erhabene* ("Die Welt als historischer Gegenstand ist im Grunde nichts anderes als der Konflikt der Naturkräfte untereinander selbst und mit der Freiheit des Menschen, und den Erfolg dieses Kampfes berichtet uns die Geschichte" [The world as a historical object is basically nothing other than the conflict of natural powers among themselves and with human freedom, and history tells us the success of this fight] (54), and posits it as the understood and assumed background of Schiller's later historical plays. Giese stresses that historical reality is to be found in the operation of different historical forces; in other words, the realism to be found in historical representation lies in the representation of this dynamic, not in the details of "who," "when," "where," and "what." Giese, like many of his colleagues, conflates history with fate; he speaks of "geschichtliches Schicksal" [historical fate] and claims that Schiller wishes to show the moments in which a hero has come to meet this destiny. He maintains that Schiller's view of history is essentially "humanistisch-idealistisch" [humanist-idealistic], going so far as to agree with Fricke that it is religious.

Hans Fabricius, author of the ominously titled monograph *Schiller als Kampfgenosse Hitlers* (Schiller as a Battle Comrade of Hitler), had no literary background; he was an administrator and lawyer. He identifies the historical element as the primary one in Schiller's dramas, works in which Schiller simultaneously painted a picture of the world and showed his concern for the welfare of the people. This aspect would render Schiller "*völkisch*" and provides one motivation for calling him "Hitler's comrade." Fabricius notes that Schiller shows the people that their forefathers have survived past events in order to demonstrate how similar events may be handled in Schiller's present, as well as in the Third Reich. Despite Fabricius's infamous title, he seems to be the critic with the most sober, least irrational or mystical view of history: the facts are there for use in the present. Fabricius, however, was mostly ignored by other critics, who viewed him as a dilettante.

Hermann Pongs, an academic who taught at Marburg, Groningen, Stuttgart, and, after the war, in Göttingen, attempted initially to connect the National Socialist beliefs in blood and race to the inner principles of art, but after 1933 he conformed to the standard National Socialist line. He is a critic who synthesizes the positions of Fabricius and Fricke in wrestling with philosophical issues as well as in a more earth-bound concern with history and his fellow human beings.

Like Fabricius, Lily Hohenstein chose a military title for her monograph: *Schiller: Der Kämpfer — Der Dichter* (Schiller: The Fighter — The Poet). Although she interweaves biographical information with her interpretations of the dramas, she allows a view of Schiller's attitude toward the historical to emerge. Claiming that Schiller had abandoned his calling as historian and philosopher with *Wallenstein,* she lauds his transformation after *Don Carlos* into a dramatist poet who grasps his heroes with emotions. In her examination of *Wallenstein* she does not always make it clear whether she is referring to the character Wallenstein or to the historical person. She mentions the historical particularly in discussing the astrological elements, maintaining that they are used for "Zeitkolorit" [period coloration] (308); she speaks of the relationship between Max and Thekla without mentioning that it is fictional. In general, Hohenstein's treatment is impressionistic and even less academic than those of her colleagues.

In his 1935 review of several publications on Schiller, Friedrich Braig-München criticizes previous readings of the playwright. He accuses Fricke of "historische[n] Relativismus" [historical relativism] in viewing the Catholic Middle Ages as a stage of human history that it was necessary to overcome. Next, he criticizes Hans Heinrich Borcherdt for superficial scholarship in according the Catholic elements in *Maria Stuart* and *Die Jungfrau von Orleans* merely aesthetic importance. Here, claims Braig-München, the critic overlooked the true forces at work both within Schiller's soul and in history. More attention should have been paid to the spiritual unity of the German people, and more intensive research on Schiller will certainly right this wrong. In so doing, the scholar will be able to bring to the surface information about historical reality and other absolute necessities (188–89). Braig-München then introduces his own reading, which posits Schiller as simultaneously dramaturge and philosopher of history whose recognition of the interplay of the historical, the tragic, and the religious moves him farther from the secular Enlightenment sphere toward the large lines of the real process of history — toward the ordering principles of metaphysical ontology. Here is where Schiller is revolutionary, says Braig-München, because he is aware of this metaphysics of poetry and history; for this reason the Christian Middle Ages, as well as the true spirit of the ancients, reveal themselves to him in a historical-tragic-religious manner (189). To confirm his position Braig-München points to Wilhelm (not Oswald) Spengler's study "Das Drama Schillers: Seine Genesis" in *Von deutscher Poeterey* (Leipzig: J. J. Weber 1932), which claims that after Schiller's intense work with historical and philosophical writing he was in a position to recognize the essentially historical and to put it to service in his dramas. Out of the "river" of history he sees human beings in their relationship to the ordering principles of the world and, thus, in their relationship to the eternal. The "eigentliche" [actual] events take place in the reconciliation with these principles. This view sounds much like Dilthey's; Braig-München and Wilhelm Spengler, however, take a religious turn in equating creation with the Creator: within this conciliation lies the dramatic character of history. In this way Spengler ties history (or perhaps historical fate) and religion together in Schiller's dramas. Braig-München's concept of history focuses on large-scale events and movements with no attention to historical accuracy, on a metaphysical, teleological development more similar to *Universalgeschichte* than to the nineteenth-century detail-oriented view.

Reinhard Buchwald, the only non-Nazi treated in this chapter, discusses Schiller's religious and moral views in his article "*Maria Stuart* und *Die Jungfrau von Orleans:* Die klassische Kunstform als Träger der sittlichen Ideen und der religiösen Symbole" (*Maria Stuart* and *Die Jungfrau von Orleans:* The Classical Art Form as Vehicle for Moral Ideas and Religious Symbols, 1941) but refers to the historical, unfortunately, only in passing. Buchwald remarks that Schiller's relationship to history as source material for his tragedies underwent changes, as did other elements in his production. He views Schiller's Wallenstein as yet another version of the figure presented in his historical writings, one that continued the attempt to solve the historical riddle of the man's motives. But later Buchwald looks for conflict-laden situations, returning to the notion of history as a treasure chest of inspiration for the historical dramatist. Regarding *Maria Stuart,* Buchwald does point to a historical inaccuracy in the Scottish queen's age, while at the same time warning against giving free rein to historical expectations when considering the play; indeed, he claims that some directors make the situation worse by tinkering with the historical aspects in order to try to make them more accurate. Buchwald often mentions historical materials, but there is never a sense that he believes that they must be treated with respect.

Franz Stuckert speaks of the rational and the irrational in *Die Jungfrau von Orleans;* he is one of the few National Socialist scholars to compare the actual events of the *Jungfrau's* life to the way Schiller re-creates them. Because Schiller does not allow Joan of Arc to end her life at the stake as a witch and, in fact, makes a radical alteration in a crucial aspect of the historical material, he is distancing himself from the religious aspect of the play (96). Stuckert sees the idea of *Vaterland* behind this drama, but also an incarnation of Schiller's notion of the *erhabene Seele* [ennobled soul] who becomes the carrier of a historical fate. Once again, history and fate are merged into one. Schiller, however, fails adequately to portray the irrational and wonderful, says Stuckert. He asks why nineteenth-century audiences most loved this drama and *Wilhelm Tell,* the plays in which one can discern Schiller's limitations most clearly. He answers that the heroic and moral pathos exhibited in these dramas speak to different parts of the German spirit; it is only in the Third Reich that these plays can be properly appreciated — not through the intellect, as in Schiller's time, but through the heart. Stuckert ends by saying that Schiller has now become history himself and is incapable of rendering a relevant model to Germans of the 1940s.

While this chapter is not by any means an exhaustive look at the Nazi era nor an attempt at theater history, it would be unthinkable to leave unmentioned the horrors that emerged from National Socialist ideology. One instance may suffice to represent the multitude. Georg Ruppelt mentions stagings of Schiller's late historical plays in Theresienstadt, the "model" concentration camp; whereas censorship was applied rigorously elsewhere in the Third Reich, little attention was paid to what went on stage in the *Konzentrationslager.* On one occasion *Maria Stuart* was performed and, in Herbert Freeden's words, "Todgeweihte spielten für Todgeweihte ein Drama, in dem die Heldin im Tode über sich selbst und über ihre Feindin triumphiert" [Condemned played for condemned a drama in which the heroine triumphs over herself and her enemy through death] (111).

Third Reich critics worked hard at appropriating Schiller, but most of what they wrote has now been forgotten; at the very least, it is no longer taken up in serious Schiller studies. Much of this criticism was simply a heaping up of rhetoric around a canonically German figure; to be sure, any systematic National Socialist approach would have been difficult in a situation where a poetics was never successfully articulated. Two critics, Fricke and Wiese, emerged into the postwar years as still viable critics, partly because they retained some scholarly integrity sandwiched between nods in the direction of Nazi ideology. The notion of history tends to be portrayed as mystical, or confused with fate, or sufficiently dealt with by a mention or two of historical inaccuracies.

The important issue is not how history and Schiller were viewed during this time, but how Schiller could be cleansed of the taint of more than a decade of Nazi contamination. This project was undertaken after the war by the builders of the GDR; what resulted will be examined in chapter 5.

Works Cited

Albert, Claudia. *Deutsche Klassiker im Nationalsozialismus: Schiller, Kleist, Hölderlin.* Stuttgart: Metzler, 1994, 48–76.

Bartels, Adolf. *Deutsche Dichter.* Leipzig: H. Haessel, 1943, 142–59.

Braig-München, Friedrich. "Das Bild Schillers in der Literaturforschung der Gegenwart," *Der katholische Gedanke* (1935): 185–96.

Buchwald, Reinhard. "*Maria Stuart und Die Jungfrau von Orleans*: Die klassische Kunstform als Träger der sittlichen Ideen und der religiösen Symbole," *Zeitschrift für deutsche Bildung* 17 (1941): 215–30.

Buchwald, Reinhard. *Wandlungen unseres Schillerbildes.* Leipzig: Liebisch, 1938.

Cysarz, Herbert. *Schiller.* Halle and Saale: Niemeyer, 1934, 309–57.

"*Das war ein Vorspiel nur...*" *Bücherverbrennung Deutschland 1933: Voraussetzungen und folgen.* Ausstellung der Akademie der Künste vom 8. Mai bis 3. Juli 1983. Berlin: Medusa, 1983, 207.

Denkler, Horst, and Karl Prümm, eds. *Die deutsche Literatur im Dritten Reich: Themen, Traditionen, Wirkungen.* Stuttgart: Reclam, 1976.

Deubel, Werner. "Umrisse eines neuen Schillerbildes," *Jahrbuch der Goethe-Gesellschaft* 20 (1934): 1–64.

Fabricius, Hans. *Schiller als Kampfgenosse Hitlers.* Berlin-Schöneberg: Deutsche Kulturwacht, 1934.

Freeden, Herbert. *Jüdisches Theater in Nazideutschland.* Tübingen: Mohr, 1964, 111.

Fricke, Gerhard. "Schiller und Kleist als politische Dichter," *Zeitschrift für Deutschkunde* 48 (1934): 222–38.

———. *Vollendung und Aufbruch: Reden und Aufsätze zur deutschen Dichtung*. Berlin: Jünker & Dünnhaupt, 1943, 353–470.

———. *Wege und Wandlungen deutscher Dichtung von Nietzsche bis zur Gegenwart*. Jena and Leipzig: Wilhelm Gronau W. Agricola, 1943, 5–11.

Giese, Rudolf. *Politische Haltung und politische Motive im Drama der Klassiker (Goethe, Schiller, Kleist)*. Hamburg and Würzburg: Richard Mayer, 1938, 51–75.

Gilman, Sander, ed. *Nationalsozialistische Literaturtheorie: Eine Dokumentation*. Frankfurt am Main: Athenäum, 1971.

Haider-Pregler, Hilde. "Das Dritte Reich und das Theater," *Maske und Kothurn* 17 (1971): 203–14.

Hohenstein, Lily. *Schiller der Kämpfer, der Dichter*. Berlin: Neff, 1940, 297–354.

Ibel, Rudolf. *Weltschau der Dichter*. Jena: Diederichs, 1943, 242–68.

Jäger, Erich. "Führer und Gemeinschaft: Eine Betrachtung im Anschluß an Schillers Wallenstein," *Zeitschrift für Deutschkunde* 52 (1938): 521–29.

Linden, Walther. *Geschichte der deutschen Literatur von den Anfängen bis zur Gegenwart*, fourth ed. Leipzig: Reclam, 1937, 310–12.

———. "Schiller und die deutsche Gegenwart," *Zeitschrift für Deutschkunde* 48 (1934): 513–31.

Nolte, Ernst. *Three Faces of Fascism: Action Française, Italian Fascism, National Socialism*, trans. Leila Vennewitz. New York, Chicago, and San Francisco: Holt, Rinehart & Winston, 1966, 3–26, 275–425.

Petersen, Julius. *Geschichtsdrama und nationaler Mythos: Grenzfragen zur Gegenwartsform des Dramas*. Stuttgart: Metzler, 1940, 1–9, 15–21, 56.

———. "Held und Volk in Schillers Drama," *Zeitung für deutsche Bildung* 10 (1934): 577–91.

Pongs, Hermann. *Schillers Urbilder*. Stuttgart: Metzler, 1935, 1–9, 21–32, 45–49.

Ruppelt, Georg G. *Schiller im nationalsozialitischen Deutschland*. Stuttgart: Metzler, 1979.

Smith, Herbert. "Present Day Tendencies in the Interpretation of Schiller," *Publications of the English Goethe-Society*, new series 11 (1935): 20–36.

Storz, Gerhard. *Das Drama Friedrich Schillers.* Frankfurt am Main: Societäts-Verlag, 1938, 119–77.

Stuckert, Franz. "Rationalismus und Irrationalismus in Schillers Die Jungfrau von Orleans," *Zeitschrift für Deutschkunde* 48 (1934): 93–106.

Vowinckel, Hans August. *Schiller — Der Dichter der Geschichte.* Berlin: Junker & Dünnhaupt, 1938, 57–127.

Werner, Karl Ferdinand. *Das NS-Geschichtsbild und die deutsche Geschichtswissenschaft.* Stuttgart, Berlin, Cologne, and Mainz: Kohlhammer, 1967, 9–97.

Wiese, Benno von. *Die Dramen Schillers: Politik und Tragödie.* Leipzig: Bibliographisches Institut AG, 1938, 64–115.

5: Schiller from the Left: Early Leftist Criticism and Criticism in the German Democratic Republic

SCHILLER'S RENOMMÉ IN Marxist circles has been, and continues to be, multivalent. On the one hand, Schiller's birth placed him in a clearly bourgeois background. Despite continued financial and physical suffering, he came into closer and more frequent contact with members of higher than of lower classes. One can describe his aesthetic project in clearly elitist terms: artists, possessing talent or insight on a higher level than the average citizen, create aesthetic experiences that critics, also in possession of superior powers, interpret for the masses. He was more interested in educating princes than in furthering of the lower classes. His stance on the French Revolution is ambivalent if not counterrevolutionary (although *Die Räuber* has been read, perhaps mistakenly, as a prorevolutionary manifesto).

On the other hand, leftist scholars since Marx, as well as cultural functionaries in the German Democratic Republic (GDR), could not unconditionally condemn or ignore Schiller because of what they might have perceived, anachronistically, as anti-Marxist tendencies. As evidenced by publication history, theater statistics, musical settings of his poems, statuary, street names, and other phenomena, Schiller has remained rooted in the German consciousness on all social and material levels. And certainly there is considerable evidence in his oeuvre of a "pre-Marxist Marxist" awareness of certain economic issues. Clearly, within a historical ideology that focuses on the lower classes, it is a far more efficient tactic to shape Schiller's works to Marxist precepts through selective criticism than to discredit him. Marxists and bourgeois critics have fought over Schiller from 1848 onward; as early as the centenary of Schiller's birth, competing Schiller celebrations were marked by ideological tensions and, in some cases, physical violence. This was, for example, the case in Berlin on November 10, 1859 (Dahlke, 13).

The problematic engagement of Schiller interpretation and Marxism begins with Karl Marx (1818–83) himself. As he and Friedrich Engels (1820–95) developed their theories around the mid-nineteenth century, they understood the need to take a stand on Schiller. His philosophical writings were more troubling than his historical dramas; since part of Marx's original project was to focus on economic issues and human suffering rather than on theoretical constructs, he reacted against Schiller's idealism, which he and Engels saw as a bourgeois escape from actual human misery into Kantian impossibilities. Additionally, Marx criticized Schiller for using human beings, especially in the historical plays, as mere mouthpieces for the spirit of the times (Dahlke, 13). Both men express disappointment over what they perceive as Schiller's lack of understanding and sympathy for the French Revolution. But they also recognize positive characteristics; Engels lauds *Die Räuber* for its revolutionary spirit, and he gives Schiller faint praise for showing tendencies toward realism, an issue crucial to Marxist criticism. Engels's definition of realism focuses on the true-to-life rendering of typical characters in typical circumstances. Such a view focuses not on historical details but on representing a true picture in its entirety. By this definition, says Engels, the content of Schiller's work qualifies him partially as a realist, while the form he uses (for example, his employment of verse) does not. Even nonrealistic forms of representation can have a certain truth content, however.

Although Engels does not apply his notion of the priority of economic development specifically to Schiller, it will return in later Marxist criticism and, therefore, needs some mention. Engels sees all human development (religious, legal, political, philosophical, literary) as subordinate to but not determined by economic development; he posits a dialectical relationship between these forms of development. In terms of Marxist-Leninist literary criticism, then, it is necessary for the critic to view his/her object in terms of historical and material issues according to the principles of "*Widerspiegelung*" [realism; the word is translated literally as "reflection"), as well as in terms of the dynamic relationship of all areas of life and work (Blumensath/Uebach, 61).

The Marxist ideas that set the basic parameters according to which literary scholarship in the early GDR judged Schiller are, then: realism (*Widerspiegelung*), economic issues as primary in the dialectic relationship of all areas of development, the education of the working class toward socialist awareness, and the ineluctable movement of history toward revolution. Before these ideas began to determine cultural policy in the GDR, they were further shaped by Lenin and Stalin. Interpreting and delineating Lenin's specific variant of realism — socialist realism — occupied GDR cultural workers and party officials for years. Indeed, one wonders in retrospect if it ever was properly and clearly defined. In its original form it incorporated two ideas: *Parteilichkeit* [the quality of being aligned with the Communist Party] and *Volksverbundenheit* [national solidarity]. *Parteilichkeit* is grounded in an allegiance on the part of the artist (in this case, the writer) to party goals and, in practice, has an educational function in inspiring great deeds, awakening the love of work, enriching the life of the mind, developing the rational and emotional faculties, and educating the people to true joy in life (Günter Mehnert, in Blumensath/Uebach, 54).

Stalin's notion of the author as engineer of the human soul comes close to this notion of *Parteilichkeit*, of the potential for the writer to change people's lives through educating them rationally and emotionally. The primary distinguishing characteristic of *Volksverbundenheit* is the prioritization of the objective interest of the people as interpreted by the party. Related to the notion of *Volksverbundenheit* is the expectation that the gap between art and the people and, consequently, between art and entertainment, is to be diminished. (By this reasoning *Volksverbundenheit* was used in the GDR as a rationale for establishing the same aesthetic standards for "belles lettres" and popular fiction.) The two concepts obviously became tightly intertwined; Mehnert explains that the true artist is able to unite them. Socialist realism, to summarize its Leninist definition, means that art no longer reflects life, but, rather, the ideal life reflects (socialist-realistic) art. As Lenin formulates the idea: "human consciousness does not only reflect the objective world, but creates it as well" (Blumensath/Uebach, 60; the original passage reads: "Das Bewußtsein des Menschen widerspiegelt nicht nur die objektive Welt, sondern schafft sie auch," W. I. Lenin, *Philosophische Hefte*, in his *Werke*, Bd. 38, 203.)

From the 100th anniversary of Schiller's death in 1905 into the 1920s leftist critics such as Franz Mehring (1846–1919), his student G. G. (Gertrud) L. Alexander, Clara Zetkin (1857–1933), and Rosa Luxemburg (1871–1919), among others, wrote literary criticism from the perspective of the working-class struggle for emancipation. These critics focused primarily on Schiller's idealism, on his revolutionary tendencies, and on the portrayal of the lower classes in his works. Much effort was spent in wresting Schiller from the grasp of bourgeois critics; no longer was criticism leveled at Schiller for being bourgeois. Because a significant portion of the KPD (Kommunistische Partei Deutschlands [German Communist Party]) functionary and literary critic Alexander Abusch's criticism takes issue with Mehring, he will be discussed in some detail.

Mehring is the first leftist literary critic after Marx and Engels who deals with Schiller in depth. He began his career as a mainstream journalist but rapidly became disillusioned by the increasingly capitalistic press in Bismarck's Prussia. He also saw corruption in theater criticism in the 1890s, when, as he saw it, money had ruined any chance for the display of true art. Thereafter, he wrote only for socialist papers until his death. Mehring advocated the study not only of the art object itself but also of its effect (reception history). In other words, he refused to see the literary work in a vacuum but advocated the study of its economic and political ramifications. Mehring sees the bourgeois class in the nineteenth century gradually relinquishing its dreams and ambitions for emancipation and in its place a more and more fervent embrace of Wilhelminian ideology. He was certain that it was only in an international socialist context, devoid of national partisanship, that critics could once again render autonomous judgments on art.

In *Schiller — ein Lebensbild für deutsche Arbeiter* (Schiller — a Biography for German Workers) Mehring sees Schiller's work and his view of the world through the limitations of the historical conditions under which he developed. He interprets the late historical plays in terms not only of events from Schiller's time but also of the fight for emancipation of the working class (Dahlke, 18). He distances himself from the picture of Schiller as a writer concerned with patriotic issues: "nichts lag ihm ferner, als die Wirkung seiner dramatischen Kunst durch die Gestaltung von 'Nationalgegenständen' zu steigern" [nothing was farther from his intent than to increase the effect of his dramatic art through the formation of 'national objects'"] (Dahlke, 157) — a stance that will anger Abusch. Mehring praises Schiller's technique of allowing historical figures to act as resonators for contemporary events; the *Wallenstein* trilogy is the best example of this technique, followed by *Maria Stuart*.

Although *Maria Stuart*, for reasons that will be discussed later, does not excite many Marxists, Mehring is more favorably disposed to it than are his later compatriots. His rationale is that the play exemplifies Schiller's keen sense of history — that Schiller was able to delineate the complicated twists and turns of the English mix of religion and politics that characterized the sixteenth century. He gives as examples Burleigh, the master of "cruel, hard, sober politics-as-business" on the side of the English Reformation, and, on the side of the European Counter-Reformation, the charm and seductiveness of the "glamour" of the arts and sciences that drove minds even colder and wiser than that of the fanatic Mortimer back into the Catholic fold. His attitude toward *Die Jungfrau von Orleans* is more negative. He thinks that Schiller did as great a disservice to Joan of Arc as did Voltaire: the German tried to solve the problem of the miraculous through the heart, the Frenchman through wit. Mehring has no patience for Schiller's "distortion" of the historical record in allowing his Johanna to mow down the enemy, on the one hand, and fall in love at first sight, on the other. The marriage proposals she receives at court are also problematic for Mehring. He points out that the historical Count Dunois wrote that neither he nor his men ever thought of her as a human woman because she was so holy. The "real" story, as it is given in the historical annals, is, to Mehring's mind, far more poetic than Schiller's play; the effect of the latter is "rein äußerlicher und theatralicher [*sic*] Art" [of a purely superficial and theatrical nature] (Dahlke, 167). Mehring seems oblivious to the implications of patriotism and the lower-class origins of the heroine, themes that will captivate GDR scholars.

The journal *Die rote Fahne* (The Red Banner) was the KPD answer to the Socialist tendency to divorce aesthetics from politics in the Weimar Republic in order to "rescue" readers who were looking for entertainment rather than political exhortation. (One can see here a precursor to the narrowing of the gap between belles lettres and entertainment literature in the GDR.) Although *Die rote Fahne* devoted many of its cultural pages to serialized and somewhat trivial novels — a genre also prevalent in bourgeois journals — the paper kept alive the connection between aesthetics and politics. Because bourgeois art, including dadaism and expressionism, was considered by leftist critics to be decayed and tainted, *Die rote Fahne* saw the critic as an educator who could train the working class to find its way to true art. This notion reminds one of Schiller's project, though his potential audience could not yet have been called "proletarian."

G. G. L. Alexander reviewed a performance of *Wallensteins Tod* in *Die rote Fahne* in December 1920. She makes a clear distinction between "revolutionary" and "rebel," claiming that Schiller focused not on the former but on the latter. Rebels are, according to Alexander, a manifestation of the positive side of Schiller's flight into art: Schiller cannot act himself, but he is able, through his art, to put humans who act — who participate in world history — on the stage. That which is truly revolutionary in Schiller is the conviction that one can only change the world through action, claims Alexander (Dahlke, 267). She is not as troubled by the astrological symbols as are later critics; she views astrology as a system of mystical laws that guide a person's behavior, laws that are as fixed as the patterns of the constellations. She sees Wallenstein sympathetically as a man whose behavior has been thus determined, a man who wished to have the crown in order to bring the peace to the world that the emperor would not.

Before examining two examples of how Schiller's late historical plays were analyzed in the GDR, let us turn to the development of cultural policy first on antifascistic and later on Marxist/Leninist/Stalinist principles, for these standards affected not only how new German literature was to be written, but also how literary criticism was expected to focus itself.

After the Second World War the Soviet Union moved quickly to purge the SBZ (*Sowjetische Besatzungszone* [Soviet area of occupation]) of all traces of Hitler's disastrous twelve years of rule, as well as to establish "Demokratie und . . . bürgerlichen Freiheiten" [democracy and freedoms for the citizens] (Blumensath/Uebach, 10) in the area. Initially the emphasis lay on the antifascist side of the equation; indeed, the years 1945 to 1949, before the establishment of the GDR, were labeled "the period of antifascistic democracy." The Nazi past was condemned not only for what Hitler had done but also for German cultural arrogance.

In June 1945 the writer Johannes R. Becher was granted permission to establish the Kulturbund zur demokratischen Erneuerung Deutschlands [Cultural Union for the Democratic Renewal of Germany]. This organization developed into the regulatory agency for literature in the GDR. One of the principles set forth in the establishment of the organization is of particular interest to the Schiller scholar: "Wiederentdeckung und Förderung der freiheitlichen humanistischen, wahrhaft nationalen Traditionen unseres Volkes" [rediscovery and promotion of the freedom-focused, humanistic, truly national tradition of our people] (Jäger, 12). This principle encouraged renewed interest in Schiller. In the opening address to the Kulturbund on July 4, 1945, the Nazi past was addressed in strong words: "In shameless, overweening self-importance, the German people were persuaded that it was the only true cultural people of the world, leading to Hitler's attempts to gain world dominion" (Blumensath/Uebach, 1*). The cultural inheritance of the German people was acknowledged to be poisoned, and its rehabilitation was considered a matter of some urgency. This program included filling the vacuum by quickly reestablishing a vital, tangible cultural and literary life; one way to do so was to reappropriate German authors who had been used in the service of the Third Reich, Schiller among them. Additionally, Soviet experts searched out German writers who had gone into external or internal exile during Hitler's regime and invited them to return for cultural work in what was to become the GDR. Becher was one of these "recruits"; he became an important figure in the establishment of cultural policy in the new communist state. The playwright Bertolt Brecht was another, but he eventually chafed under the restrictiveness of party regulation. In October 1949 the GDR was founded, and work was begun, under the aegis of the *Kulturbund,* to formulate cultural policy according to Marxist/Leninist/Stalinist principles.

The policy statement of the newly reformed KPD, explicated by party official Anton Ackermann, betrays an ominous tenor beneath the idealistic, encouraging words. He speaks of freedom for science and art, assuring scientists and artists that they do not need to worry about party affiliation or press censorship. But then he begins to speak about "Pseudokünstler" [pseudoartists]: if they attempt to cast mud on freedom, democracy, or the idea of the community of people, they shall feel "das gesunde Volksempfinden" [healthy public feeling], as will "pseudoscientists" who try to do the same (quoted in Jäger, 9–10). The ominous tone can be attributed partly to Ackermann's use of Nazi vocabulary ("pseudo-," "gesundes Volksempfinden") but also to the suspicious vagueness surrounding the notion of "Pseudokünstler." This room for interpretation will be used later in the establishment of a repressive cultural policy.

The basic contradiction in GDR cultural policy from its beginning in 1949 has been explained by the scholar Manfred Jäger as a conflict between communist ideology and the desire to privilege art beyond institutional strictures, thereby granting it a freedom that the citizens and society in general were not permitted (150). The socialist enterprise is a collective activity, and much of the effort expended by the party and the *Kulturbund* was directed at bringing writers and other artists into the group-oriented venture. But if artistic creation is an individual activity — and one for which not all members of a collective have suitable talent — it is not surprising that a tension will develop between the ideal and the real.

By September 1, 1951, the idealistic tone of the founding principles of the *Kulturbund* had changed. During a speech given at the establishment of the Amt für Literatur und Verlagswesen [Bureau of Literature and Publishing], Ministerpräsident Otto Grotewohl made it clear that even literary works of high artistic quality — including literary criticism — must be rejected when their tendencies are reactionary. In other words, political criticism is primary, artistic freedom secondary (Jäger, 35–36). In July 1952 the Second Party Congress of the SED (Sozialistische Einheitspartei Deutschlands [Socialist Unity Party of Germany]), in accordance with its decision to build a socialist state in the GDR, mandated that writers employ socialist realism. This approach reflected Leninist doctrine: writers were to become socialist heroes, educating the people along the path to socialism, "engineering souls." Reflection of party policy and patriotic ideals (*Parteilichkeit* and *Volksverbundenheit*) took precedence over "artistic freedom" — indeed, artistic freedom was repudiated as a reactionary bourgeois notion. How socialist realism was to be implemented in practice remained vague, but the *"positive Held"* [positive hero] provided one concrete guideline. Not only would this hero show strength, stability, and socialist consciousness in the present; he or she would display belief and optimism in looking toward the future. It is no wonder that GDR critics felt drawn to Schiller's larger-than-life heroes as prototypes for these characters.

As is the case with many theories, socialist realism had little success in practice. By July 1953 East German intellectuals were feeling handcuffed by the limitations of the doctrine. Proposals for giving authors more autonomy were laid before the SED; little action was taken, and Brecht, among others, reacted violently. Brecht declared that "der Schrei nach Lebendigem ist . . . ein Schrei nach Lebendigem für Särge. Die Kunst hat ihre eigenen Ordnungen" [the call for the living is a call for coffins. Art has its own principles] (542). Although the state claimed that it wanted artists, it wanted them only under conditions that killed the artistic impulse. Anna Seghers (1900–1983) echoed this sentiment three years later when she said that these conditions gave rise to paralysis rather than movement, laziness instead of initiative; the readers of books written according to the principles of socialist realism will not be moved at all (Jäger, 78). The authorities briefly and vaguely expressed sympathy toward the intellectuals in an attempt to appease them; the death of Stalin in 1953 and the events in Hungary in November 1956, however, led to an environment that was even more repressive than before.

By 1959 cultural functionaries, while not responding directly to complaints along the lines of Brecht's and Seghers's pleas, decided to try a new approach to socialist realism, one that leaned more heavily on the notion of *"Volksverbundenheit"*; this decision resulted in what became known as the "Bitterfelder Weg" [Bitterfeld Way], named for the location of the GDR writers' conferences at which it was developed and proposed in April 1959 and April 1964. This new direction in authorship, reminiscent of workplace writing groups early in the century, meant that all workers were to become writers and all writers workers. Misgivings about the project expressed by some writers at the second conference were dismissed by the authorities, who said that the times demanded a party-focused rather than a "free" art. Though some intellectuals suggested classifying socialist realism as a *Weltanschauung* — a move that would allow more creative leeway — it was made into its own aesthetic category in 1962, and its fate was thus sealed. Socialist realism had stifled creativity; by the mid-1960s writers had ceased to attend writers' conferences, and the split between artists and party officials was deep and wide. The field of literature became sterile and far from an effective tool for socialist education.

How was Schiller to be handled in the new republic? The first step, naturally, was to rehabilitate him from the Third Reich tradition that had used him for its own ends. In the July 4, 1945, statement by the Kulturbund zur demokratischen Erneuerung Deutschlands mentioned above Schiller is named as one of the true German cultural treasures, along with Goethe and Lessing. Speeches claiming Schiller as a proletarian hero abounded, especially in the Schiller jubilee years 1955 and 1959. Some of the rhetoric included appropriate citations from Schiller's work — for example, "Seid einig, einig, einig" [be united, united, united], from *Wilhelm Tell*. (The practice of putting winged words from Schiller's plays into a completely opposite context from the original was continuing: these words are spoken by the nobleman Attinghausen, who is no proletarian; the play itself is far from ambivalent in exploring the possibility of true democracy.)

The next step was to find a way to install Schiller as a proper model for socialist literary critics and writers. Although the tendency to claim him as an ally in the fight for emancipation of the working classes was strong, some ambivalence was initially apparent. Members of the radical left felt that Schiller and, in fact, German Classicism as a whole were "bloße Reproduktion des bürgerlichen Erbes" [mere reproduction of the bourgeois inheritance] (Blumensath, 10). This minority opinion was soon overcome, however, and literary critics were free to work with Schiller — as long as they paid heed to party standards. In 1959 the GDR celebrated its tenth anniversary, and the sentiment that East Germans and not West Germans had both the right and the proper ideological orientation to appreciate Schiller was strengthened. The GDR functionaries accused the West of neglecting Schiller as antiquated and unmodern and claimed that the West, because of its militarism and indulgence in political intrigues, could not understand what the GDR loved about Schiller. A speech given at the SED celebration of the 150th anniversary of Schiller's death sees in Schiller's dramas, poetry, and prose works a union of humanity and patriotism that moves the people — both present and past generations — to greatness and love of freedom.

The speech was given by Alexander Abusch, a literary critic and party functionary who believed that East Germany had a higher moral claim to Schiller because it was not beholden to corrupting capitalist/imperialist motives. He was also one of the greatest critics of writers and thinkers who did not align themselves with party policy — for example, he actively denounced Georg Lukács, Ernst Bloch, and Hans Mayer. The criticism that will be examined here is taken from Abusch's *Schiller: Größe und Tragik eines deutschen Genius* (Schiller: Greatness and Tragedy of a German Genius, 1965). By way of comparison a 1960 collection of essays by the academics Edith Braemer and Ursula Wertheim, *Studien zur deutschen Klassik* (Studies in German Classicism), will be included in the discussion. Abusch tends to push Schiller into the party mold; Braemer and Wertheim, who were not party functionaries, are more willing to see Schiller as a product of his times and less likely to strain their interpretations. Hans-Günther Thalheim focuses primarily on class issues surrounding feudal systems and capitalism. Because his reasoning is much in line with Abusch's, he will not be examined in detail. All of the critics address issues of realism (which includes *Volksverbundenheit*), economic development and repression, and education of the masses toward socialism and revolution.

The *Wallenstein* Trilogy

The *Wallenstein* trilogy finds more resonance with GDR scholars than either of the other two plays examined in this study. It speaks to all three of the socialist concerns just mentioned: realism, economic issues, and education toward socialism and revolution. GDR scholars have seen *Wallensteins Lager* as the first portrayal of working-class or peasant characters who raise their voices and make a claim to power. The depiction of starving peasants (the farmer and son with the loaded dice) and foot soldiers qualifies as realism, and the references to the material and emotional devastation wrought by sixteen years of war set up the economic background of the trilogy and foretell Wallenstein's eventual fall. Wallenstein himself is viewed in a positive light as a revolutionary and a leader concerned with uniting the German-speaking world rather than as a blatant opportunist.

Abusch sees *Wallenstein* as a "Nationalepos" [national epic] (1965, 225). He finesses Marx and Engels's complaint about Schiller's flight into the realm of the ideal by claiming that Schiller fought against his own idealism, that the revolutionary wrath, the pure feelings, and the patriotic hopes of his people can be traced in the pathos of his works. Abusch clearly wishes to rewrite history to claim Wallenstein as a proletarian champion. He leaves the framework of the play to look ahead to the end of the Thirty Years' War, at which time, because of Wallenstein's ruin, German-speaking lands were in worse shape than ever (222). He quotes a letter to H. Meyer (June 6, 1797) in which Goethe says that Schiller used the contemporary story of Dumouriez as background for the play, thus leaving behind the historical Wallenstein in favor of a presentation of current events. While Abusch does not go so far as to say that the play supports the French Revolution, he claims that Schiller was sympathetic to the ideas of national unity that the revolution represented (246). The critic idealizes Wallenstein's undertaking, seeing high patriotism in the general's resistance to allowing the Swedish forces to take over. Wallenstein's tragedy lies in his lack of understanding and in the actions he takes — or does not take — in accordance with this obtuseness. Abusch says that Schiller uses Euripidean tragedy, where a man falls not through the play of fate but by his own actions — a step closer to realism than Sophoclean tragedy, which Abusch finds more mystical. Schiller thus showed that poetry and realism are not opposites in a great work of art. For Abusch, Max and Thekla serve the function of counterweight to the realistic Wallenstein — they are characterizations of *Anmut und Würde* [grace and dignity] and thus not realistic; Max, however, redeems himself as an incarnation of the "national idea," and, as a patriot, comes closer to the sphere of the realistic than does Thekla.

Schiller introduces the trilogy with the appearance of two peasants; Abusch reads this staging as evidence that Schiller wished to remind the audience of historical events preceding the Thirty Years' War (the Peasant War, the Hussite unrest) that had already brought those living in German-speaking lands at the beginning of the seventeenth century to a state of economic ruin. But Abusch finds the astrological apparatus suspect and claims that Goethe steered Schiller wrong in suggesting it. He complains that it prevents the presentation of economic conditions in the empire from bearing fruit; although Schiller began to set forth such a presentation (the appearance of the farmer in *Wallensteins Lager,* Questenberg's mention of the unrest in all classes and the Kellermeister's remembrance of his Hussite background in *Die Piccolomini*), nothing in *Wallensteins Tod* continues this line: the astrological elements take over here. He thinks that Schiller should have highlighted Wallenstein's potential function as peace-bringer for the merchants — the main power behind early capitalism — whose trade had been interrupted by the Thirty Years' War (245).

Abusch, too, subscribes to the notion that Schiller did well to change historical facts and to invent figures in order better to express the "große[n] Geschichtsbegebenheit" [greater events of history] (246). Some critics would see a split between the portrayal of ideals in history and the portrayal of actual events, but Abusch refutes the notion that this play is an idealization. He ascribes the pathos of patriotic ideals that is spoken by such figures as Max not to an impulse to idealize but to the nature of a realistic work of art in which idealistic human beings fight for progressive ideas.

Abusch claims that bourgeois literary critics tried to hide the historical implications of the play by calling it a tragedy of immorality. Instead, he claims that Wallenstein's guilt lies not in immorality but in the fact that he is stuck in a feudal, absolutist, Bonaparte-determined mindset and thus isolates himself arrogantly instead of acting decisively and quickly against the "Ewiggestrigen" [a term from the trilogy that is difficult to translate; it means literally "eternal yesterday," and one senses that he is referring to an antiquated way of thinking]. Wallenstein should have acted as a national leader — and here Abusch uses the tainted term *Führer* — who knows how to synthesize the aims of the army with the interests of the city dwellers and peasants (246). He blames Schiller for muddying the waters by implying that Wallenstein was misled into treachery by the siren of power. This comment exemplifies Abusch's tactic of finding elements that conform to party cultural policy and suggesting improvements to the play where Schiller's text does not support socialist ideals.

Jost Hermand claims that work on German classicism in the GDR falls into one of two categories: either it is positivistic and avoids discussions of theoretical issues, or it tries to lend the primary literature a greater political relevance (Marxist, naturally) than it previously had (135). Edith Braemer and Ursula Wertheim, while making a case for greater political relevance, do not do violence to Schiller in the process. Braemer and Wertheim see in Schiller an individual artist who, through precisely this individuality, fulfills the requirements of realism. Schiller adheres to a concept of realism that is not formalistic and chronology-based but qualitative and aesthetic, which is appropriate for artistic realism. This statement indicates a desire to consider Schiller's project deeply and impartially while staying within the confines of party policy.

Braemer and Wertheim consider *Wallensteins Lager* groundbreaking in the way it portrays members of the lower classes. The delight the soldiers take in plundering their middle- and lower-class compatriots and the disdain they feel toward their victims result from their deprived economic background. The action of the play thus turns largely on an economic axis: the economic situation of the soldiers. The play is also the first in German literature to portray the common man as part of a greater, potentially powerful group that can change the course of history. The potential for such a play to awaken revolutionary awareness in citizens of the GDR is obvious.

Like Abusch, Braemer and Wertheim view the unhistorical Max Piccolomini as a realistic figure, a political progressive — not as the embodiment of "schöne Seele" [beautiful soul] that many West German scholars, including Benno von Wiese, do. His mind is focused on peace, they claim, not only for himself but for all "die unter der Last des Krieges seufzenden Bürger und Bauern" [the city dwellers and peasants sighing under the burden of the war] (195). In their reading he is more surely a *positiver Held* than is Wallenstein himself. He is not merely a product of Schiller's poetic fantasy but was created directly out of eighteenth-century history; he is a pre-Enlightenment rationalist who has characteristics of a patriotically-minded *Bürger* of the eighteenth or nineteenth century. Braemer and Wertheim ignore Max's inability to understand his contemporary world politically and focus on his goals for the future. His inability to achieve these goals is a function of history and not of

Max's unrealistic, idealistic mindset. He is seen as a man before his time, defeated in the present but victorious in the future.

The notion of a united Germany — an important political and emotional issue for the GDR — seems to have pressed GDR scholars to project Wallenstein as the hero who could have unified the country in the seventeenth century. Abusch couches this wish in terms of peace-seeking; Braemer and Wertheim say that Wallenstein cannot agree to cooperate with the Swedes because doing so will not only fail to bring peace but will also make unifying Germany impossible (195). On the other hand, despite the obvious ideological advantage of perceiving Schiller as strictly *volksbunden* [patriotic], Wertheim cites a letter to Körner that makes nationalizing Schiller problematic: this is the letter of October 13, 1789, in which Schiller says that it is a "pitiably small idea to write for *one* nation; for a philosophical mind this limitation is completely unbearable" (quoted in Braemer and Wertheim, 159). She allows readers to decide how this comment should affect one's interpretation of Schiller's desire to see a united Germany.

The astrological elements are downplayed by Braemer and Wertheim as much as they are by Abusch. Instead, historical and political elements lead, in combination with Wallenstein's hesitancy, to the general's downfall. Wallenstein had to fail, according to these critics, because of his failure to act decisively in the class struggle between feudalistic absolutism, symbolized by the emperor, and the new bourgeois social order promoted by Max.

Braemer and Wertheim return frequently to the theme of revolution. One of Wertheim's essays in the collection refers to Schiller's interest in the American Revolution and how it was discussed at the Karlsschule (105). She also mentions the *Bauernkrieg* (Peasants' War), ideologically important to the GDR, in comments on Goethe's *Götz von Berlichingen* (164). She makes this connection between Schiller and revolution explicit in discussing his reaction to the French Revolution. Until his death, she claims, he struggled with the events of the revolution, attempting to come to clarity about them; all of his late plays bear witness to this struggle. In this way she stops short of declaring Schiller a revolutionary but allows for a revolution-focused interpretation of his plays without categorically arguing for one. (Nearly twenty years later Helmut Koopmann will see *Wallenstein* as a veiled history of the French Revolution itself, but he will claims that Schiller questions the viability and meaningfulness of human action because the revolution fails.)

Maria Stuart

Scholars in the GDR, as well as Marxist scholars in general, have focused most frequently and extensively on the *Wallenstein* trilogy and *Die Jungfrau von Orleans*. This focus should not be surprising, for while the lower-class characters in *Wallensteins Lager* are primarily positive, the misery of the farmers forced to support Wallenstein's armies is portrayed at least fleetingly, and Johanna is seen as a folk hero of humble origins, *Maria Stuart* provides no positive proletarian element. The heroine is of royal birth; the conflict revolves around her and another queen; and the only characters who remotely resemble proletarians are Maria's servants, none of whom exhibit revolutionary tendencies or maltreatment by their mistress. Instead, they are more loyal to their queen than they are to each other. Queen Elizabeth, in fact, in referring to "her" people, displays anti-lower-class sentiment in at least two instances. At Fotheringhay she expresses a desire to elude them ("Das Volk drängt allzuheftig in den Straßen, / Wir suchen Schutz in diesem stillen Park" [The people are crowding much too fiercely in the streets, / We shall seek shelter in this quiet park]) (III, 4). She refers to them either with slight repulsion or with distrust, describing them as "wankelmütig" [capricious] or comparing them to a weak reed ("Wehe dem, / Der auf dies Rohr sich lehnet!" [Woe to him, / Who leans on this reed!]) (IV, 11).

Abusch wastes little time on *Maria Stuart;* he spends a mere three and one-half pages on it (compared to just over twenty-five on the *Wallenstein* trilogy and nine and one-half for *Die Jungfrau von Orleans*). He condemns the play for lack of historical accuracy in the portrayals of both queens. He says this not because of the fictional meeting between them or of the invented characters such as Mortimer: he is critical because Schiller has misinterpreted history, wrongly seeing in the developments in England parallels to the story of Wallenstein. He points out that Elizabeth played a progressive role in English history. Abusch says that Mehring erred in claiming that Schiller was a historical prophet and that Mehring, like Schiller, failed to see that what is important is whether one acts as a progressive or as a reactionary. He thinks that Schiller was wrong in painting a black picture of so progressive a queen as Elizabeth and was wrong in making Maria, who had no potential to become a great and progressive leader, a heroine. As he did for *Wallenstein,* he suggests improvements to the play, wanting Schiller to have made Elisabeth's contributions more visible and her sympathy and help for her people more tangible. The emphasis on Elizabeth's legitimacy is thus a flaw, and Abusch ignores the crucial tension this question supplies for Schiller's drama. Braemer, too, has little to say about this play, and what she does say is negative. She mentions only that Schiller had had to fight with the historical material in both *Wallenstein* and *Maria Stuart* and that the latter play, especially, was a variation on current problems in negative form. All three critics, disagreeing with Mehring, are clearly more excited about Schiller's "romantische Tragödie," *Die Jungfrau von Orleans.*

Die Jungfrau von Orleans

The choice of a peasant girl as nationalist heroine has obvious positive implications for a Communist audience. The GDR critics tend to ignore the fact that Johanna, despite repeated mentions of her lowly origins, shows little interest in the lower classes, turning her attention instead to the court, which gives her a noble title that she does not refuse. (Braemer does note, however, that Johanna refused all noble suitors, guessing that she was anxious to return home.) She is far more interested in her calling, though her relationship to the Virgin Mary is interpreted by Abusch as a metaphor for her patriotism.

From Abusch *Die Jungfrau von Orleans* earns praise — surprisingly — for its commitment to realism. He compares the inactivity of the French leaders to the situation in Germany around 1800: he sees the disappointment the German people felt about the defeat of the emperor and his generals during Schiller's time as the background against which Schiller imposes the encouraging story of the rise of France against England. This situation parallels postrevolutionary, centralized France, in whose interest it lay to keep Germany split and impotent; Abusch used the same reasoning in his analysis of *Wallenstein.* He takes issue with Mehring for denying any "modern-nationale Tendenzen" (259) in *Die Jungfrau von Orleans;* to him it is clear that Johanna is a peasant girl representing her people on the stage of world history and involved in forging a nation. He sees Johanna's "religious" call as a romantic disguise for a drama about defense of homeland, independence, and national unity. In the weak and hesitating king and court saved by a peasant girl, Abusch infers Schiller's conviction that in situations of political and historical crisis the power of the lower classes was essential — for example, during the French Revolution. As if to dispel any lingering suspicion that Schiller was less interested in real history than in mysticism in the play, he admits at the end of his analysis that Schiller himself was dissatisfied with *Die Jungfrau von Orleans,* in part because of the contradiction between strong realism and fantastic mysticism, but never had the opportunity to rewrite the play.

Abusch believes that the public reacted to this drama with great enthusiasm not because of the stunning theatrical effects but because they saw their own patriotic feelings mirrored in the play, and these feelings needed a proper outlet during a time of such shame for Germany. Unlike Mehring, he finds Johanna's fictionalized death on the battlefield a truer historical result than if the facts had been represented more accurately: she dies with her soldiers, further tightening the identity between Johanna and the French people.

The revolutionary content of the play is obvious to Abusch. *Die Jungfrau von Orleans* could not be staged in Weimar; the reason traditionally given is that the duke of Weimar did not want to see his mistress, Caroline Jagemann, in the role of Joan of Arc. Abusch believes that this explanation is a bourgeois invention and that the real reason it could not be staged there was because of the play's revolutionary implications. He interprets the contemporary popularity of the French "Heldenlied" [heroic song] and the fact that people shouted "Es lebe [Long live] Friedrich Schiller" after the first act of the third performance of *Die Jungfrau von Orleans* as evidence that the people understood this revolutionary content.

Braemer begins her analysis of *Die Jungfrau von Orleans* from a different point, though the degree of realism in the play is also of interest to her. She quotes the letter to Goethe in which Schiller claims to have triumphed over "das Historische" and explains that by "triumph" Schiller meant that he had extracted the essential from history, leaving behind that which was merely incidental.

What he meant by "essential" was primarily "naive" themes that had to do with the appearance of the girl herself. Braemer, like Abusch, points to the historical parallels between France in the fifteenth century and northern Germany in Schiller's time. But she also mentions the ambivalence Schiller surely felt in turning to the problematic western neighbor for inspiration. The two poles of this ambivalence are, naturally, the French Revolution and the defense of France against foreign invaders in the fifteenth century. Braemer sees this ambivalence played out outside the drama in terms of historical issues that had to do with how the class struggle took shape in France both during the time of Joan of Arc and at the end of the eighteenth century. In Germany this struggle could not take the same form during Schiller's time; German conditions could not support a bourgeois revolution. Braemer, however, sees an alternative parallel: a compromise was anticipated in Joan of Arc's time between the bourgeoisie and the nobility in which the nobility would voluntarily become part of the bourgeoisie. The period of early absolutism was thus a good model for the anticipated union between the two classes in Germany; for this reason Schiller emphasized the aspect "mit Vehemenz" [vehemently] in his tragedy (222).

Braemer refers to several historical inaccuracies in the play: Johanna's mission includes not only the historical routing of the English but also the unification of France (an issue with obvious connections to the twentieth-century desire for German unification); the French rejection of Johanna is better explained in the drama than in the historical materials; she falls in love with an English soldier; her death comes on the battlefield rather than at the stake. But she is quick to point out that these deviations from historical accuracy do not jeopardize the truthfulness of the drama. Schiller is still a realist for reasons that have to do with aesthetic considerations. There is a clear distinction between "Fabel" [plot] and "Handlung" [action]. Braemer calls on the Aristotelian definition of each term: plot is an artistic weaving of events, action is plot in the greater context of characterization and motives. Braemer explains that the choice of the material, the creation of the story, and the action in its entirety, including the plot, are the three stages of the "Widerspiegelungsprozess" [reflection process] (note the use of the Marxist term) that finally result in a unified whole. This analysis is certainly applicable to the historical drama (230). She points out that one can create a poetic "Fabel" that corresponds closely to the historical materials, while veering radically from history within the context of the "Handlung." In this way, for example, the reconciliation of France and Burgundy, while accurate in the "Fabel," becomes inaccurate in the "Handlung" because Schiller places this event, though true, in incorrect historical sequence in relation to the crowning of the Dauphin and Johanna's death.

Braemer next addresses two events that do not occur even in the "Fabel": Johanna's love for Lionel and the appearance of the Black Knight. These she sees as necessary for the play to speak its truth. Johanna's love for Lionel is a sin not because she has broken her vow but because she has committed treason. In allowing herself to feel love for the enemy, she has failed to be sufficiently patriotic. Braemer cites lines from IV. 1 in support: "Kümmert mich das Los der Schlachten, / Mich der Zwist der Könige? / . . . / Doch du rissest mich ins Leben, / In den stolzen Fürstensaal, / Mich der Schuld dahin zu geben, / Ach! es war nicht meine Wahl!" [Was I concern'd with warlike things, / With battles or the strife of kings? / . . . / But thou didst send me into life, / 'Midst princely halls and scenes of strife, / To lose my spirit's tender bloom: / Alas, I did not seek my doom!] (Schiller, 95). Johanna's fall is also related to her departure from her "proper place." In assuming a position of power she makes herself vulnerable to the threat of corruption; this threat can be circumvented only if Johanna remains immune to personal ties. Only without such ties can Johanna maintain her crucial connection both to the world of the lower classes and to the court.

Braemer interprets the second element not supported by either the historical record or the use of the *Fabel/Handlung* dichotomy, the Black Knight, as a romanticizing element that shatters the previous sense of reality and mirrors the unrealistic conviction on Johanna's part that she has received a divine calling. The Black Knight's appearance draws attention to that conviction and foreshadows Johanna's eventual realization that she is human; her death on the battlefield with her soldiers, although historically inaccurate, represents the triumph of reality and confirms Johanna's status as folk hero.

Economic issues do not take prominence in this play, but Braemer mentions Schiller's association of Johanna with Minerva as evidence that such issues were at least subliminally present. Schiller envisioned a copper engraving of the goddess on the title page of the play; since Minerva was the goddess not only of war and philosophy but also of domestic work, Braemer infers a view of the equality of all human pursuits before capitalism forced workers into dehumanizing specialization.

This play says more about socialist education than about economic development. Braemer sees Thibault's disapproval of his daughter's project as a reactionary warning against rebellion rather than as a familial reproof. Involvement in national affairs is the concern of the king and the nobility, not of the lower classes, at this time. Because Johanna's rebellion is successful, however, it provides an example that even king and nobles must acknowledge. It is this rebellion that Braemer calls "das eigentliche 'Wunder'" [the true "miracle"] in the play — that a humble shepherdess takes it upon herself to work both outwardly (against the English) and inwardly (toward national unification); it is a miracle emerging from the early Enlightenment, when the king was still seen as a protector of his subjects and the provider of a security within which the people could gain self-consciousness. Johanna emphasizes this view of the monarch by warning the king against losing the people's trust, for in such a case he is no longer fulfilling his proper kingly role. This warning, of course, echoes the events of the French Revolution: "Der Hochmut nur kann ihn zum Falle führen, / Und von den niedern Hütten, wo dir jetzt / Der Retter ausging, droht geheimnisvoll / Den schuldbefleckten Enkeln das Verderben" [Arrogance can only lead him to a fall, / And from the lowly cottages, from which to you now / The savior issued, threatens mysteriously / Destruction on the guilt-marked grandchild] (III, 4). Braemer realizes, at the same time, that she is dealing in anachronisms here and refers to the religious aspect of the play. The first roots of a national consciousness, she argues, must in the fifteenth century have found their origins in a religious consciousness, not a political one. Schiller must have known this fact and taken it seriously; he was able to work the religious and the political together without resorting to anachronism.

Braemer sees the rejection Johanna experiences from her family and the French court as a result of Johanna's progress. She has come so far that her people can no longer follow her. As she regains her voice and proclaims her innocence to Raimond (the one character who understands the pull of both family and world history), she returns to self-confidence and a belief in the truth. She finally dies in battle, covered with the banners of her nation, and is thus reunited with France, the nation she has helped to establish. Braemer's theory about Schiller's decision to rewrite Johanna's death — despite adherence to the sources elsewhere — brings the play into line with socialist realism. Although an accurately portrayed death at the stake would satisfy Johanna's individual need to atone, it would not heal the breach between Johanna and her people. The fictionalized ending on the battlefield, in the arms of her comrades, gives a final tableau of national unity. As such it conforms to the future-focused requirement of socialist realism — that an example of the utopian postrevolutionary state be presented on stage as a perceivable if not yet attainable reality. As Braemer explains, Schiller could not employ a concretely historical portrayal; he had to find an artistic way to explode the framework of reality (269).

Braemer identifies other revolutionary aspects in the play besides Johanna herself, notably the use of the word *Hütte* [cottage]. She sees the cottage as the site of solidarity between "Bürgern, Bauern und Plebejern" [bourgeois, peasants and plebeians] in rebellion against the oppressive nobility, and though by 1800 this topos had largely lost its power in German literature because of disillusionment with the French Revolution, Schiller rehabilitates the idea by emphasizing Johanna's humble origins and by staging her as the force that emerges from the lower classes to lead the nation. Braemer joins the realistic aspect of the play to the revolutionary by calling attention to Schiller's choice of a peasant heroine and claiming this choice as evidence of a new level of realism. This stage is higher than simple realistic portrayal, for it is an aesthetic reflection of a societal development in which the active involvement of the lower classes in building the nation becomes acknowledged as necessary. This aesthetic reflection, in turn, expands the national consciousness (226–27). Braemer places Schiller's Johanna on a par with the revolutionary women in Paris in the 1790s and in contemporary Mainz ("die jakobinisch gesinnten Frauen von Mainz" [the Jacobin-minded women of Mainz]) (227). And in noting Schiller's choice of France and a heroine of humble origins Braemer, like her colleague Wertheim, can associate Schiller with the French Revolution without inaccurately designating him a supporter of it.

Schiller's rearrangement of chronology (Burgundy's reconciliation with France occurs in the play before the victory over the English and during Johanna's lifetime) adds to the revolutionary content of the play. Braemer sees a pressing concern for internal unity; in fact, for her the reconciliation scene is the climax of the play politically, for it paves the way for a French nation-state. National unity is imperative during a time when the lower classes and the bourgeoisie are not strong enough to strike out on their own, when they still need the help of the king and the nobility not only in France (both in Johanna's time and during the French Revolution) but also in contemporary Germany. She maintains that Schiller staged an example of how revolution could be carried out in nineteenth-century Germany. Braemer goes so far as to maintain that Schiller was showing direct support for revolution. She ties the revolutionary aspect of the play to the realistic with one last firm knot: she avers that the representation (she uses the word *Widerspiegelung*) of a historical fight for freedom, as well as of its principal actress, emerges from such a strong sense of being in the present that the metaphysical questioning is incapable of touching the realistic content (262). This move, it can be argued, brings her in line with Abusch's allegation that Schiller would have rewritten the play, but it is a more sophisticated (and less suspect) tactic than his.

While Abusch, Braemer, and Wertheim all address party and Marxist issues and see socialist concerns mirrored in Schiller's works, Braemer and Wertheim do so in thoughtful and convincing ways. Braemer's argument about *Die Jungfrau von Orleans* is especially persuasive and sophisticated. All three critics convey the belief that Schiller was instrumental in putting members of the lower classes on stage in the role of acting, speaking, and suffering humans for the first time in German literary history. But he has gone one step further: he has proven that he is aware of the lower classes' historical power, of their potential to change the course of history. For this reason they see in him an awareness of *Volkstümlichkeit* that rejects any criticism of his alleged elitism. In *Wallenstein* and *Die Jungfrau von Orleans, positive Helden* are supplied for a socialist audience in the form of Max Piccolomini and Johanna (and, Abusch maintains, of Wallenstein himself). In short, these critics make effective motions to pull Schiller to the left, making him a viable Marxist dramatist. In the case of Braemer and Wertheim one begins to wonder if, indeed, Schiller were not more experimental than critics previously claimed him to have been. More than one West German critic, while arguing from a different point of view, will agree with them.

Works Cited

Abusch, Alexander. *Schiller: Größe und Tragik eines deutschen Genius.* Berlin and Weimar: Aufbau, 1965, 209–88.

———. *Schillers Menschenbild und der sozialistische Humanismus.* Berlin: Aufbau, 1960.

Berman, Russell. "Literary Criticism from Empire to Dictatorship, 1870–1933," in Peter Uwe Hohendahl, ed. *A History of German Literary Criticism, 1730–1980.* Lincoln and London: U of Nebraska P, 1988, 277–357.

Blumensath, Heinz, and Christel Uebach. *Einführung in die Literaturgeschichte der DDR.* Stuttgart: Metzler, 1975.

Braemer, Edith, and Ursula Wertheim. *Studien zur deutschen Klassik.* Berlin: Rütten & Loening, 1960, 189–296.

Brecht, Bertolt. *Gesammelte Werke,* vol. 19. Frankfurt am Main: Suhrkamp, 1967, 542.

Dahlke, Günther, ed. *Der Menschheit Würde: Dokumente zum Schiller-Bild der deutschen Arbeiterklasse.* Weimar: Arion, 1959, 9–25, 37–39, 51–56, 120–22, 156–67, 196–210, 241–81, 293, 306–9.

Demetz, Peter. *Marx, Engels and the Poets: Origins of Marxist Literary Criticism,* transl. Jeffrey L. Sammons. Chicago and London: U of Chicago P, 1967, 107–15, 127–30, 152–59, 178–89, 226.

Hermand, Jost. *Geschichte der Germanistik.* Reinbek bei Hamburg: Rowohlts Enzyklopädie, 1994, 114–40.

Jäger, Manfred. *Kultur und Politik in der DDR 1945–1900.* Cologne: Edition Deutsche Archiv, 1995.

Koopmann, Helmut. "Die Tragödie der verhinderten Selbstbestimmung: Schillers Aufklärungsdenken, die französische Revolution und Wallenstein als politische Antwort," in Koopmann, ed. *Freiheitssonne und Revolutionsgewitter: Reflexe der Französischen Revolution im literarischen Deutschland zwischen 1789 und 1840.* Tübingen: Niemeyer, 1989, 13–58.

Schiller, Friedrich. *The Maid of Orleans, The Bride of Messina, Wilhelm Tell, Demetrius, The Piccolomini, The Death of Wallenstein, Wallenstein's Camp,* transl. Sir Theodore Martin, Anna Swanwick, A. Lodge, and Samuel Taylor Coleridge. London, Berlin, and New York: Robertson, Ashford & Bentley, 1902.

Wellek, René. *A History of Modern Criticism, 1750–1950: German, Russian, and Eastern European Criticism, 1900–1950.* New Haven and London: Yale UP, 1991, 64–115.

6: The Federal Republic of Germany and Post-(re)unification Criticism

WHILE GERMANS LIVING in the Soviet occupational zone set to work after the Second World War to construct a nation founded on Marxist-Leninist principles, their former compatriots in the British, French, and American zones developed a capitalist democracy closely supervised by the occupation forces. The Federal Republic of Germany (FRG) was founded on May 23, 1949, largely as a counterforce to the Soviet Bloc. This new nation shared a cultural and intellectual legacy with the GDR that transcended political and ideological differences. Both nations acknowledged the need to reclaim the common cultural inheritance and cleanse it of the taint of the Nazi past. Their methods of doing so differed, however, and the clash between them set the tone for Schiller criticism in the early postwar years. The tug-of-war reached a climax between the jubilee years 1955 and 1959 — the same period during which the East-West borders were finally stabilized.

Ironically, in wresting Schiller from the grasp of the Third Reich both sides resorted to similar methods in attempting to lay the better claim. Markus Michel wrote an essay titled "Schiller the NATO-Poet?" in 1959; Johannes R. Becher went so far as to say that the GDR, with Soviet help, was about to bring the German tragedy to its peak of perfection, a task initiated by Schiller. The battle was fought within the theaters, as well. The East German critic C. Funke, reviewing a GDR production of *Wallenstein,* could assume that the audience understood the general's significance for national unity. The audience also enjoyed the political implications of the play and had no need for the Western "aesthetics of shock and excitement," as Funke expressed it (264). In the West, the "freedom" in Schiller's epithet "poet of freedom" was interpreted to mean the freedom to be unpolitical.

The results of two devastating world wars were a sense of confusion, loss of universal truths, and loss of the possibility of absolute objectivity. This mood comes to the fore in the attitude toward historiography in the FRG, where different reactions to the events of the twentieth century are evident. While East German political consciousness revolved around Marxist tenets, West German society was marked by a withdrawal from political issues, especially in literature and literary criticism. It was not until the 1960s that politics returned to importance in literary circles. Before that time, productions of and critical essays about Schiller's late historical plays tended to the psychological. It was not until the mid 1980s, when the historical novel began to see a resurgence of popularity, that Schiller was reevaluated in terms of the historical implications of his plays.

But a beginning was made in the 1970s. After the renewal and revolution of the 1960s a broader spectrum of political opinions arose in the following decade, providing reasons to reexamine Schiller's politico-historical tragedies. As has been the case throughout this study, *Wallenstein* garnered the most interest. Walter Mueller-Seidel, without intending to do so, opened the discussion in 1971 with a new political interpretation. Mueller-Seidel shows how Wallenstein stands in a dynamic relationship to the established order, while Octavio Piccolomini becomes a rigidified enforcer. According to Mueller-Seidel, *Wallenstein* made apparent an experience of history that was new at the time: an actual witnessing of the unfolding of change. Another aspect of newness occurs in the introduction of a new "realm of peace" to take the place of the antiquated imperial one. Mueller-Seidel's second, and greater, *Wallenstein* study (1976) makes one aware of the elements of epic theater in *Wallensteins Lager*. To be sure, the feel is episodic; there is no peripeteia, no climax in this "prologue" to the main action of the trilogy. Brecht's indebtedness to Schiller is clear, perhaps never more so than when one compares a staging of *Wallensteins Lager* with, for example, *Mutter Courage*. Mueller-Seidel ties the belief in astrology with Wallenstein's belief in destiny, and he interprets the drama as a process of cognition/perception and tragic analysis (365).

In an article in the same issue of the *Jahrbuch der deutschen Schillergesellschaft* as Mueller-Seidel's second study, Christiaan L. Hart-Nibbrig tries to tie in this play more firmly with Schiller's aesthetic project. Hart-Nibbrig shows that Schiller's reflections about history as "Sinn- und Handlungszusammenhang" [a context of reason and action] (257) have led to questions about action in history and its relationship to the possibility of aesthetic representation. Schiller must have set Wallenstein up as an example of a poor citizen of the aesthetic state. He cannot find his way from freedom of play to free action and is stuck in his aesthetic education. Hart-Nibbrig pushes aside concerns about the realism versus idealism in the play to make a case for *Wallenstein* as an example of aesthetic interpretation of history.

At the end of the decade yet another possibility is voiced. Walter Hinderer proposes focusing on the illusions in the play that are destroyed by the end. It is not the positive action of history that is at stake; rather, it is reaction to events. In pointing to the ways in which interpretations of astrological signs (and historical events) can lead one astray, the drama exemplifies how one must interpret history in multiple ways rather than attempt to single out one simple truth.

Postmodern theories begin to gain ground in West Germany in the 1980s as well. The reaction to them is not completely positive. The critic Jürgen Eder, for example, voices dismay over the promotion of a vague existentialist rhetoric helped along by the domination of methods of analysis that deal primarily with form and structure rather than with content. This approach, he says, forms an antithesis between the tragic failure of the individual and the collective (Koopmann, 785). To be sure, historicism still holds sway in some camps, where history is seen as a scientific discipline; in others there is a realization of the necessity to turn to other disciplines — psychology, sociology, and folklore, to name just three — to find help in rendering a useful picture of the past. The flooding of the intellectual community with a range of possible interpretations and disciplines that can be applied to literature seems overwhelming, however. The eminent Schiller scholar Helmut Koopmann attributes the lack of longer monographs on Schiller, the flourishing of essay collections, and the tendency of scholars to monologize and speak past each other instead of engaging in exchanges of opinion — all of which he finds detrimental to scholarship — as symptoms of the widening of possibilities.

In the most recent decades the literary-critical approach known as New Historicism has renewed interest in the examination of how history is portrayed and has aroused suspicion on the part of historians, who see their enterprise cast into doubt. In the new Germany, Hayden White's *Metahistory* has not yet met a full critical challenge, according to Wolfgang Weber; most German historians have merely ignored it. Some, including Jörn Rüsen, see in New Historicism a return to Ranke's acknowledgment of historiography's debt to literary forms (Fulda, 8). This claim, of course, does not go as far as White's notion that the historian performs a poetic act that prefigures the historical field in which the rules for representing history are developed. The dependence of history on language and the consequences of this dependence are, however, issues that can no longer be ignored in German critical circles.

Daniel Fulda asks if the traditional opposition between Enlightenment thought and historicism cannot be resolved through a return to aesthetics, rhetoric, poetics, and narration and their reception by historians (11). In other words, why should historians be afraid of turning to these fields if they have already turned to others (psychology, etc.) for assistance? As Richard J. Evans points out, Ranke himself was indebted to philology (8). In response, Dietrich Harth turns the question on its head and asks what the function of rhetorical, stylistic, and poetic apparati can be in the design of a consistent (Harth uses the German *konsistent*) picture of history "in dem Sinne ... daß sie sowohl zentrale Faktoren der historiographiegeschichtlichen Entwicklung auszuleuchten verspricht als auch die Sinnbildungsleistung und damit kulturelle Funktion der Geschichtswissenschaft komplexer zu sehen erlaubt" [in the sense ... that it as well as central factors in historiographical-historical development promise to enlighten as well as allows us to see the emblematic accomplishment and therewith the cultural function of the study of history with greater complexity] (Fulda, 13). To add to the range of possible outcomes of this argument, Ulrich Muhlack argues that historiography and historical perception, or historiography and the "science" of history, are, in actuality, identical.

While it would seem a natural move to connect Schiller to New Historicism, it has not been done yet in any significant way. Rüsen speaks of New Historicist theories specifically in regard to Schiller and mentions the "Gestaltungskraft" [power of representation] that authors use to form historical knowing; it is this power that comes across as primarily poetical or rhetorical. And Eder makes Schiller sound like the most radical of New Historians: "Schiller wird ... vom Künstler beeinflußt, indem er die scheinbare, nur vordergründige Wirklichkeit der Fakten (Überlieferung ist auch

Herrschafts-Geschichte, Geschichte der 'Sieger') durchstößt und nach Möglichkeiten, Alternativen, dem Anderen fragt" [Schiller is . . . influenced by the artist, as he penetrates the apparent, merely foregrounding reality of facts (transmittal is also history of those in power, the history of the "victors") and asks about possibilities, alternatives, the other] (Koopmann, 657). This comment brings to mind Michael André Bernstein's term *counterlives,* events that did not happen; as Bernstein explains the concept:

> A prosaics of the quotidian requires a willingness to remain receptive to the voices from the shadows in order to safeguard itself from becoming either a new kind of reductionism or a blind affirmation of whatever has triumphed sufficiently to flourish in the glare of actuality. Counterlives count because they are a constituent element of the lives we have, just as it is often by the shadows the sun casts, not by its direct light, that we can best calibrate where we stand. . . . (7–8)

Though Bernstein is here applying his notions of counterlives and sideshadowing specifically to literature of and about the Shoah, they are useful for example, in studying *Maria Stuart* in a postmodern context. They move the debate past the well-worn struggle with Schiller's historical blasphemy in putting two queens who never met onto the stage at the same time to a dynamic interaction between possibilities. Schiller's continued interest in revolutionaries and other usurpers can be seen in this light. His fascination with the "flashpoints" of history, the changing of systems and the distribution of power, must indicate an awareness of alternate possibilities. Indeed, this awareness is exactly what Claudia Albert attributes to Schiller: an ability to step outside of the limits of the possible.

In this connection Schiller has been held up by several West German critics as being more experimental than his reputation allows. One such critic is Helmut Koopmann, who recognizes Schiller's experimentation with historical materials in particular. Montage is one technique that Koopmann claims Schiller used frequently, not merely with historical materials and his own creation but also within his ideas. The amalgamation of heterogeneous materials that becomes apparent in his work, his ability to synthesize radically opposed concepts, and his versatility in working with different genres all point to abilities not generally possessed by his contemporaries (xvii). He points specifically to *Die Jungfrau von Orleans* as one of the most experimental plays written by Schiller or any of his contemporaries.

We now turn to the criticism surrounding the late historical plays during the 1980s and 1990s, primarily in Germany. Otto Johnston, an American critic, is included because the 1980s brought an increase in the acceptance of work by Anglo-American scholars. He points out that *Wallenstein* has been thoroughly examined for its indebtedness to historical sources, but that few have looked to what is thematized in the play. He mentions Goethe's explication of the figure Dumouriez behind Wallenstein and adds his own observations; for example, Buttler's dialogue with Gordon (*NA* 8, IV, 2, 6, 8) in *Wallensteins Tod* show many points of contact with the reports that Danton and Lacroix sent to the National Assembly during their reconnaissance trips to Belgium. Johnston shows that Dumouriez, like Wallenstein, is able to keep the opponent's agents at bay so long that the most extreme measures must be employed to defeat the traitor. Johnston points out, however, that an important difference is that Dumouriez allied himself with the old order against the new, whereas Wallenstein wished to usurp the power of the old order.

In looking at *Maria Stuart* Johnston points out the anachronistic nature of the psychological interplay of the public and private spheres and finds them more suited to the middle of the eighteenth century than to Mary Stuart's time. The legal questions of her time recede into the background behind such issues pertinent to Schiller's day as conspiracies, corruption, and the relationship between power and conscience. In raising the question of legitimacy, which was certainly important in Mary Stuart's day, Schiller drew his audience into a powerful and painful examination of the question in their own time (Schulz will agree with this position). While Maria bases her claim to the throne on feudal laws of inheritance, Elizabeth bases hers on democratic grounds: delegation, achievement, majority, and popularity. Even the reverence of her subjects makes her a more legitimate ruler. In this way Schiller has given a historical view of the decline of the older form of government and the rise of a new one, one that Schiller does not necessarily support. Indeed, in leaving Elizabeth alone and abandoned at the end of the play he expresses some doubt about this form of government, for it differentiates between political office and private person "but only in order to all the more craftily erase the borderline between public welfare and self interest and to promote personal advantage in the political arena" (in Koopmann, ed., 59). Schiller thinks that any belief that the personal and political can be divorced is naive; where the governmental apparatus is located in the hands of a group striving for power, personal advantage will always be at stake. Johnston reminds us that the meeting of the two queens is not Schiller's invention: other playwrights had staged such a meeting; what is completely Schiller's is Elisabeth's hypocritical position vis-à-vis "das Volk." Elisabeth further distances herself from her people by seeing Maria face to face but not pardoning her; royal custom demanded such an act of mercy.

Any reader in our time who has doubts about Schiller's look to his own present, says Johnston, should remember Maria's imperious words to Elisabeth in act III: "Denn ich bin euer König" [For I am your King]; not motivated by rhythm or rhyme, the use of the masculine form is a clear indication that Schiller is thinking about the imprisoning of Louis XVI and his murder in 1793. Johnston mentions Schiller's historical sources, not only to prove the connections of incidents in the play to events of the French Revolution but also to make a case for Schiller having worked closely with the sources; in so doing Johnston reminds us of critics both from Schiller's time and from the nineteenth century.

In *Die Jungfrau von Orleans,* on the other hand, Johnston finds a movement diametrically opposed to that found in *Maria Stuart.* While Maria moves toward her divine destiny, Johanna moves toward her individuality — a point brought up earlier by Hoffmeister. An additional debt to Hoffmeister is seen in Johnston's statement that the play is historical in its creation of the supernatural mood of the Middle Ages; Johnston, however, goes one step further and claims that Schiller took his Johanna out of this supernatural mood to provide a counterweight to Voltaire's degraded "pucelle." Like Marxist critics in the GDR, Johnston sees in Johanna a patriotic figure, the first one in French history, who calls her people to arms against the common enemy. Although he does not have as much to say about Schiller's use of sources in this play, he does mention that one can see traces of his planned drama about Charlotte Corday in Johanna. This drama, then, like *Maria Stuart,* has ties to the French Revolution.

Helmut Koopmann prefaces his own analyses of the late historical dramas by reminding us of Schiller's playfulness and experimental interest. Schiller was not interested in representing reality, claims Koopmann, nor was he interested in creating psychological portraits, as Benno von Wiese and Emil Staiger would have it. Rather, Schiller engaged in a playful melting together of separate character traits that did not attempt to hide their ancestry (140). Schiller ascribed to a playful intertextuality, and it is to this intertextuality that Koopmann refers in speaking about the montage technique. He also reminds us that Schiller was not interested in a true-to-source representation of historical figures. Schiller's study of Greek tragedians and of Greek and Roman historians led him to find a bridge between true history and the poetic fable; he saw Greek tragedy as such a bridge. *Wallenstein* has certain parallels to Greek tragedy but comes across, says Koopmann, more as a modern historical drama. In *Die Jungfrau von Orleans* Schiller finally leaves the conventions of antique tragedy and develops a new form of historical drama, in this case a "legend drama" that conquers history.

Hartmut Reinhardt's essay on *Wallenstein* gives a broad view of prior criticism of the play. He comments that *Wallenstein* is emblematic of the way Schiller views the relationship of humans to politics and history. He refers to Alfons Glück's essay of 1976 in which Glück speaks of the hour that decides Wallenstein's fate — an admission that historical fact is key in *Wallenstein.* (Stephanie Barbé Hammer will give the issues of time in the trilogy a particularly eloquent expression in the cleverly titled "Schiller, Time and Again.") Reinhardt also points out that Aristotle helped Schiller to organize the extensive historical materials by confirming that he should place the greatest emphasis on the dramatic plot. Reinhardt repeats something said at least twice before about the play — that it was Schiller's attempt to bring the antique tragedy into modern times. But he puts a different spin on it, seeing Machiavellian politics in the place of the Greek oracle.

The question of fate emerges often in discussions of *Wallenstein,* often antagonistically to history. Reinhardt sees an inextricable relationship between the two. In a society or epoch that no longer supports a mythological worldview, he notes, one asks if there is a moral meaning behind the outcome of destiny. In the case of Schiller, this destiny expresses itself as nemesis. Reinhardt goes on to discuss nemesis and its relationship to history: one possibility is that nemesis is a force that rules history. As example Reinhardt turns to the Pappenheimer scene, reminding us that it is often used as evidence that Wallenstein was a peacemaker and promoter of a new form of government. He sees Wallenstein, instead, as a crafty manipulator and strategist. The former critics, says Reinhardt, fall as much prey to Wallenstein's silver tongue as the character had hoped the Pappenheim soldiers would. Herbert Kraft had expressed a more negative cast to this argument in 1974 when he said that the hero runs aground on the shoals of history and that the drama showed the fate *of* history.

Reinhardt goes on to speak of the relationship between this tragedy and Schiller's essay "Über das Erhabene" and claims that Alfons Glück is the only previous critic to have dealt with this relationship. Tragedy is bound to impart a certain moral culture, according to this essay, and in Schiller's words, "[s]ie kann und soll, wenn sie sich an die Geschichte hält, negative Exempla 'der unaufhaltsamen Flucht des Glücks, der betrogenen Sicherheit, der triumphirenden Ungerechtigkeit und der unterliegenden Unschuld' nicht vermeiden" [it can and should, when it holds itself to history, not avoid giving negative examples "of the ineluctable flight of happiness, betrayed security, triumphant injustice and defeated innocence"] (*NA* 21, 51). Reinhardt notes that it is easy to see why the sublime and its relationship to historical drama are no longer as interesting in our time, when Schiller is seen as too ideal, as they were in earlier times.

In discussing *Wallenstein* in a historical context Reinhardt notes that the play hardly qualifies as "historical drama" in the sense that Glück meant in his study of the relationship of *Wallenstein* to "Über das Erhabene." Schiller did not see history as a series of events but as his famous maxim describes it, "the conflict of natural forces among themselves and with human freedom." Reinhardt turns to possible connections to the French Revolution. It is not a play about Napoleon, but Goethe may have been right in finding traces of Dumouriez. Reinhardt is concerned with possible historical points of contact, not with the specific ways in which Schiller molds the historical material. He mentions the legitimacy problems brought up in Otto Johnston's discussion of *Maria Stuart,* agreeing that they are symptomatic of late eighteenth-century concerns. Reinhardt points the way for future research on *Wallenstein* by noting that political issues in the play have not been examined thoroughly enough by recent critics; the message of political regeneration, in particular, should spark interest in German scholars.

The prominent literary critic Gerhard Storz published a monograph on Schiller in the anniversary year 1959. He does not take any particular attitude toward the historical in Schiller's historical plays. His *Der Dichter Friedrich Schiller* (The Poet Friedrich Schiller) is characterized by its concern not with the historical or the political but with the inner structures of the works; he examines the "Formgebung" [shaping] of Schiller's creative production and deals only marginally with the historical and philosophical writings. He makes a case for not seeing Schiller as a political writer at all.

For Gerhard Schulz, questions of legitimacy come to the fore. This issue is more frequently raised in discussions of *Maria Stuart* and the question of the true line of succession. Schulz points out that this concern for legitimacy in the time of Wallenstein is actually a masked concern for the same issue in Schiller's time. But beyond legitimacy, Schulz sees in the transformation of Schiller's historiographical treatment of the Thirty Years' War into the *Wallenstein* trilogy a more intense focus on individuals, which is, according to Schulz, a sign of turning to literature. Schiller's play psychologizes Wallenstein and brings him into the present. In support of this argument, Schulz cites the discussions between Goethe and Schiller about the differences between the epic and the drama, in which they agreed that the epic describes events that are completed, while drama should make the events seem completely present; in *Wallenstein* history is brought inside the actors in order to portray it as if it were ongoing. Therefore, for Schulz, the issue at stake in *Wallenstein* is not history but the human reaction to the tension between passion and order and between nature and reason (118).

Schulz says that in the main, Schiller followed the historical facts as well as they were known in 1797. Wallenstein's guilt should be explained from the perspective of problems of legitimacy, for he betrays the legitimate power of the emperor, although he wished to serve his own greatness as well as the German nation by means of such treason; therefore, he is a "border figure in an era of change and transition" (128) who violates two different moral concepts at the same time.

The historical aspects of *Maria Stuart* have received little attention in recent decades. Gert Sautermeister provides the only exception during the 1970s: he points out that the main actors are women in a male-dominant society. Sautermeister thinks that this feature is a conscious attempt on Schiller's part to comment on gender relationships, particularly because he refers to traditionally feminine qualities such as beauty. Sautermeister views the interactions of the queens as a struggle in which neither woman achieves her initial goal. History proves itself impossible to steer and a showcase for suffering and decline. For Sautermeister, the play shows the redemptive power of art, which has taken the place of religion, and follows Schiller's theories about education through the aesthetic. He thinks that this play is not an answer to the French Revolution but is to be interpreted as an exemplification of how art allows one to transcend and ascend.

Like *Maria Stuart*, *Die Jungfrau von Orleans* was overlooked for the most part by critics in the 1980s in terms of its relationship to history and historical issues. During that time little was written on the play at all except for Claudia Albert's study. After outlining the historical sources and dealing with structural matters, she relates the play to Schiller's philosophical writings, as well as to his feelings about the French Revolution. She makes Schiller's historical experiences responsible for the fact that this play contains romantic elements, and she calls Schiller an advocate for stepping outside the limits of the possible.

Published in 1998, Karl Guthke's article for the *Schiller Handbook* is by far the most incisive, original look at the late historical plays in recent scholarship. In his discussion of *Maria Stuart* he turns immediately to the historical aspects of the play. He sees history as a panorama unfolding behind the highly dominant main characters in this play, as well as in *Die Jungfrau von Orleans*. Of course, there is interplay between the two; nevertheless, the main conflict of these dramas is played out within the characters themselves. He will, however, not relegate history to a back seat: the sweep of history remains the central issue in the play. Historical elements do not pale behind the personal, although German criticism has tended to see an Aristotelian prioritizing of the poetic over the historical in the plays. Guthke makes a foray into non-German criticism to comment on the work by Lesley Sharpe and Francis John Lamport that accord history vital importance. He notes Lamport's suggestion (also made by Johnston, another non-German critic) that the fictitious meeting of the queens is "accurate" in its portrayal of the historical conflict between two concepts of government and dominance (the feudal system versus constitutional monarchy). This symbolism constitutes "historical tragedy," according to Lamport. Instead, Guthke says, one should think of *Maria Stuart* as an interpersonal drama in which the historical has its own function: "that personal action and inability to act, often akin to a political chess game, are determined by the same forces that determine history. It is these forces that are recreated during the course of the drama" (Koopmann, 416–17).

Guthke takes some space to deal with the origins of the play and Schiller's thoughts about its historical impulses; he mentions the seeming contradiction between Schiller's wanting a historical subject and yet wanting to overcome the historical within it, and also mentions Schiller's notion of a "mittleres Genre" [midway genre] somewhere between the poetic and the historical that would unite the advantages of both. In the case of this play, Schiller did make Maria more and Elizabeth less sympathetic than he would have had he followed the sources more faithfully. One more in a long line of critics who list the liberties Schiller took with historical fact, Guthke points out that Maria never admitted complicity in Darnley's death. Schiller made these alterations for the sake of autonomous artistic composition and the portrayal of characters.

Guthke's analysis of *Die Jungfrau von Orleans* begins by asking if the play is relevant today, referring to G. B. Shaw's famous pronouncement that Schiller's Johanna had nothing in common with the historical figure — indeed, nothing in common "any mortal woman that ever walked this earth," and that the ideal words she spoke did not make her any more sympathetic to any viewer. Guthke breaks a lance for Schiller's Johanna, however. Making note of the trouble many critics have had with the contradictions and riddles in the text, Guthke dismisses many of them as part and parcel of the world of the Middle Ages and the world of the Greeks. He reminds us that Schiller treated this subject much more freely than he did Mary Stuart and did so after making half-hearted historical studies in preparation. Guthke mentions the historical *Umdichtungen* [rewritings] such as Johanna's death on the battlefield and particulars of her life itself. Part of the deviation lies in Schiller's concern with the conflict between idealistic hero and "megalomania and the complex of being a selected one"; for this reason he changed history so that his character could continue the struggle seen in such figures as Marquis Posa and Wallenstein.

In the scene in which Johanna takes up the sword one more time, against her vows, Guthke sees an act of political and individual liberation. He claims that Schiller's Johanna emancipates herself from the historical Joan; this thought is new in that it gives the dramatic character a sense of initiative and removes Schiller's hand in it. The bloodthirstiness of Johanna, for example, is not historical, but Guthke seems to welcome it. And in an ending that is perhaps the most shocking example of Schiller's manipulation of historical fact, Guthke reminds us, Johanna is still rising into a French heaven, because the banners that cover her are patriotic, not religious. In sum, Guthke pleads for an interpretation of this work that does not exclude the historico-political; he urges the reader to understand that Schiller has not simply given us a drama about a divine mission but also one about one of the issues most pressing to him: the collision of idealism and power. There is no better place to witness this collision than in political situations throughout history, including today.

One of the most recent studies on the relationship between history and poetics in *Wallenstein* was published by Theo Elm in 1996. He finds it surprising that Schiller's historical plays were so well received when his historical writings were not. He cites several scholars (beginning with Dilthey, continuing with Srbik, and ending with Schieder) who have seen Schiller's psychological portrait of Wallenstein as the author's true contribution to history. Because Schiller's historiography tended to crystallize around individuals like Wallenstein and Gustav Adolf, this view is not an unreasonable one. Elm goes on to speak about critics who have written about art and historical truth and the ways in which they conflict in the tragedy. Schiller fought with the Wallenstein material, which is evidence that he was not seeking to render a historical portrait of the general. Elm asks for a more theoretically engaged look at terms used less self-consciously than is possible in the postmodern — which "historical truth" is meant? How can what passed for historical truth in Schiller's day be applicable to us today? He admits that he has asked open-ended questions, but he supplies a strategy for finding a solution that sounds Hegelian: he begins with the conflict of the historian with the poet in the *Geschichte des Dreißigjährigen Kriegs*, continues on to the transmittal of poetic fiction and historical information in *Wallenstein,* and transcends and envelopes both issues in the function of literature as historiography in general. He turns to Hayden White and other New Historicists for assistance.

In leaving questions open for solutions by other scholars — and perhaps not only by scholars — Elm asks for participation from others. This request in itself is a new move in a community of scholars that, as Jost Hermand argues, has become increasingly isolated. In a strongly worded statement, Hermand decries the academic community as it exists today. He claims that although in an ideal world professors are engaged in witnessing, professing, and making a contribution to society through ideas, in reality many faculty members feel that they are replaceable and increasingly unimportant and allow themselves to be caught up in the hectic tempo of their publication timetables. In such a situation they can hardly move themselves to be true critics of society or to be social activators (228). Returning to look at Schiller's original project — the education of society by means of art — it seems that there is a call to action embedded in it, no matter how many aspersions are cast by critics who see Schiller's misgivings about the French Revolution as a call to mere reflection. In the past two decades some critics have fled into a theory not comprehensible to others; each postmodern practice has its own jargon. New Historicism, in its concern for viewpoints previously unexplored in traditional historiography, provides a venue for the critic to work as social activist. Hermand calls for a mode of criticism that does not focus primarily on intellectual structures that serve to build up the ego of the individual critic (he names as such discourses the psychological-existential and the formalist-aesthetic) but brings critics together into a dialogue in the building of a socially-oriented approach. To this end he singles out New Historicist and environmentally oriented criticism, as well as cultural studies. This proposal is an open one, much like Elm's, but it is an exciting one. If critics turn to Schiller's late historical plays with different issues in mind than applying obfuscating discourse, one may well return to Schiller's original ultimate project — to improve society by means of the aesthetic.

Works Cited

Albert, Claudia. *Friedrich von Schiller, "Die Jungfrau von Orleans."* Frankfurt am Main: Diesterweg, 1988.

———. "Schiller im 20. Jahrhundert," in Helmut Koopmann, ed. *Schiller-Handbuch.* Stuttgart: Körner, 1998, 773–94.

Bernstein, Michael André. *Foregone Conclusions: Against Apocalyptic History.* Berkeley: U of California P, 1994.

Bohn, Thomas M. Review of *Wissenschaft aus Kunst: Die Entstehung der modernen Geschichtsschreibung 1760–1860,* by Daniel Fulda. *Comparativ* 7, no. 4 (1997): 112–13.

Eder, Jürgen. "Schiller als Historiker," in Helmut Koopmann, ed. *Schiller-Handbuch.* Stuttgart: Körner, 1998, 653–98.

Elm, Theo. "'Ein Ganzes der kunst und der Wahrheit.' Zum Verhältnis von Poesie und Historie in Schillers *Wallenstein*," in Hans-Jörg Knobloch and Helmut Koopmann, eds. *Schiller heute.* Tübingen: Stauffenburg, 1996.

Evans, Richard J. *In Defence of History.* London: Granta, 1997.

Fischer, David Hackett. *Historian's Fallacies: Toward a Logic of Historical Thought.* New York, Evanston, and London: Harper & Row, 1970, 155–57.

Fulda, Daniel. *Wissenschaft aus Kunst: Die Entstehung der modernen Geschichtsschreibung 1760–1860.* Berlin and New York: De Gruyter, 1996.

Funke, Christoph. *Schillers "Wallenstein," Regie Solter, Deutches Theater.* Berlin: Henschelverlag, 1982, 264.

Guthke, Karl. "Die Jungfrau von Orleans," in Helmut Koopmann, ed. *Schiller-Handbuch.* Stuttgart: Körner, 1998, 442–65.

———. "Maria Stuart." In Helmut Koopmann, ed. *Schiller-Handbuch.* Stuttgart: Körner, 1998, 415–41.

Hammer, Stephanie Barbé. "Schiller, Time and Again." *German Quarterly* 67, no. 2 (1994): 153–72.

Hart-Nibbrig, Christiaan L. "'Die Weltgeschichte ist das Weltgericht': Zur Aktualität von Schillers ästhetischer Geschichtsdeutung," *Jahrbuch der Deutschen Schillergesellschaft* 20 (1976): 255–77.

Hermand, Jost. *Geschichte der Germanistik*. Reinbek bei Hamburg: Rowohlts Enzyklopädie, 1994, 141–245.

Hinderer, Walter. "*Wallenstein.*" In Hinderer, ed. *Schillers Dramen: Neue Interpretationen*. Stuttgart: Reclam, 1979, 126–73.

Johnston, Otto. "Schillers politische Welt," in Helmut Koopmann, ed., *Schiller-Handbuch*. Stuttgart: Körner, 1998, 44–69.

Koopmann, Helmut, ed. *Schiller-Handbuch*. Stuttgart: Körner, 1998, xv-xviii, 137–54, 785, 809–932.

Kraft, Herbert. *Das Schicksalsdrama: Interpretation und Kritik einer literarischen Reihe*. Tübingen: Niemeyer, 1974, 19–24.

Mueller-Seidel, Walter. "Die Idee des neuen Lebens: Eine Betrachtung über Schillers *Wallenstein*," in P. F. Ganz, ed. *The Discontinuous Tradition: Studies in German Literature in Honour of Ernest Ludwig Stahl*. Oxford: Clarendon, 1971, 79–98.

———. "Episches im Theater der deutschen Klassik: Eine Betrachtung über Schillers *Wallenstein*," *Jahrbuch der Deutschen Schillergesellschaft* 20 (1976): 338–86.

Oellers, Norbert. "Poetische Fiktion als Geschichte: Die Funktion erfundener Figuren in Geschichtsdramen Schillers," in Otto Dann, Norbert Oellers, and Ernst Osterkamp, eds. *Schiller als Historiker*. Stuttgart and Weimar: Metzler, 1995, 205–17.

Reinhardt, Hartmut. "Wallenstein," in Helmut Koopmann, ed. *Schiller-Handbuch*. Stuttgart: Körner, 1988, 395–414.

Sautermeister, Gert. "*Maria Stuart*," in Walter Hinderer, ed. *Schillers Dramen: Neue Interpretationen*. Stuttgart: Reclam, 1979, 174–216.

Schulz, Gerhard. "Schillers *Wallenstein* zwischen den Zeiten," in Walter Hinck, ed. *Deutsche Geschichtsdramen: Interpretationen*. Frankfurt am Main: Suhrkamp, 1981, 116–32.

Storz, Gerhard. *Der Dichter Friedrich Schiller*. Stottgart: Klett, 1959.

Wiese, Benno von. *Die deutsche Tragödie von Lessing bis Hebbel*, third ed. Hamburg: Hoffmann & Campe, 1955, 221–64.

Works Cited

Primary Sources

Works by Schiller:

The Maid of Orleans, The Bride of Messina, Wilhelm Tell, Demetrius, The Piccolomini, The Death of Wallenstein, Wallenstein's Camp, trans. Sir Theodore Martin, Anna Swanwick, A. Lodge, and Samuel Taylor Coleridge. London, Berlin, and New York: Robertson, Ashford & Bentley, 1902.

Schillers Werke: Nationalausgabe, 43 vols. Weimar: Hermann Böhlaus Nachfolger, 1943 -. Cited as *NA.*

Friedrich Schiller: An Anthology for Our Time. In New English Translations and the Original German. New York: Ungar, 1959.

Critical Works:

1800

Süvern, W. *Ueber Schillers Wallenstein in Hinsicht auf griechische Tragödie.* Berlin: Kölnische Realschule.

1838–42

Hoffmeister, Karl. *Schiller's Leben, Geistesentwicklung und Werke im Zusammenhang.* Stuttgart: Balz.

1852

Tieck, Ludwig. *Kritische Schriften,* vol. 3. Leipzig: Brockhaus.

1859

Rönnefahrt, J. G. *Blätter aus der Naturgeschichte der Menschheit. Drittes Blatt: Schiller's romantische Tragödie Die Jungfrau von Orleans.* Leipzig: Dyk.

1861

Rönnefahrt, J. G. *Blätter aus der Naturgeschichte der Menschheit. Viertes Blatt: Schiller's Trauerspiel Maria Stuart.* Leipzig: Dyk.

1881

Düntzer, Heinrich. "Schillers *Wallenstein,*" in his *Erläuterungen zu den Klassikern,* vols. 17–18. Leipzig: Wartig.

1882

Braun, Julius, ed. *Schiller im Urtheile seiner Zeitgenossen.* Berlin: Luckhardt.

———. ed. *Schiller und Goethe im Urteil ihrer Zeit.* Berlin: Luckhardt.

[Because both works were published in the same year, they are cited, respectively, as "Braun S" and "Braun SG."]

Bulthaupt, Heinrich. *Dramaturgie der Classiker: Lessing, Goethe, Schiller, Kleist*, vol. 1. Oldenburg: Schulzesche.

1884

Düntzer, Heinrich. "Schillers *Jungfrau von Orleans*," in his *Erläuterungen zu den Klassikern*, vols. 50–51. Leipzig: Wartig.

Ueberweg, Friedrich. *Schiller als Historiker und Philosoph.* Leipzig: Reissner.

1885

Düntzer, Heinrich. "Schillers *Maria Stuart*," in his *Erläuterungen zu den Klassikern*, vols. 19–20. Leipzig: Wartig.

1886

Rönnefahrt, J. G. *Blätter aus der Naturgeschichte der Menschheit. Sechstes Blatt: Schillers dramatische Gedicht Wallenstein.* Leipzig: Dyk.

Tomaschek, Karl. *Schiller's Wallenstein.* Vienna: Carl Gerold's Sohn.

1908

Bellermann, L. *Schillers Dramen: Beiträge zu ihren Verständnis*, 3 vols. Berlin: Weidmann.

Ludwig, Otto. *Ludwigs Werke*, vol. 4. Berlin, Leipzig, Vienna, and Stuttgart: Bong.

1912

Strich, Fritz. "Schiller. Sein Leben und sein Werk." In *Schillers Sämtliche Werke*, vol. 13. Berlin: Deutsche Buch-Gemeinschaft.

1920

Berger, Karl. *Schiller, Sein Leben und seine Werke.* Munich: Beck.

1927

Korff, Hermann August. *Geist der Goethezeit: Versuch einer ideellen Entwicklung der klassisch-romantischen Literaturgeschichte.* Leipzig: J. J. Weber.

1928

Kommerell, Max. *Der Dichter als Führer in der deutschen Klassik: Klopstock, Herder, Goethe, Schiller, Jean Paul, Hölderlin.* Berlin: Bondi.

1929

Borcherdt, Hans Heinrich. *Schiller: Seine Geistige und künstleriche Entwicklung.* Leipzig: Quelle & Meyer.

Raff, Helene. "Wallensteins Max," *Westermanns Monatshefte* 73, no. 146: 173–78.

1933

Dilthey, Wilhelm. *Von deutscher Dichtung und Musik.* Leipzig and Berlin: Teubner.

1934

Cysarz, Herbert. *Schiller.* Halle and Saale: Niemeyer.

Deubel, Werner. "Umrisse eines neuen Schillerbildes," *Jahrbuch der Goethe-Gesellschaft* 20: 1–64.

Fabricius, Hans. *Schiller als Kampfgenosse Hitlers.* Berlin-Schöneberg: Deutsche Kulturwacht.

Fricke, Gerhard. "Schiller und Kleist als politische Dichter," *Zeitschrift für Deutschkunde* 48: 222–38.

Linden, Walther. "Schiller und die deutsche Gegenwart," *Zeitschrift für Deutschkunde* 48: 513–31.

Petersen, Julius. "Held und Volk in Schillers Drama," *Zeitung für deutsche Bildung* 10: 577–91.

Stuckert, Franz. "Rationalismus und Irrationalismus in Schillers *Die Jungfrau von Orleans*," *Zeitschrift für Deutschkunde* 48: 93–106.

1935

Braig-München, Friedrich. "Das Bild Schillers in der Literaturforschung der Gegenwart," *Der katholische Gedanke:* 185–96.

Pongs, Hermann. *Schillers Urbilder.* Stuttgart: Metzler.

1937

Linden, Walther. *Geschichte der deutschen Literatur von den Anfängen bis zur Gegenwart,* fourth ed. Leipzig: Reclam.

1938

Buchwald, Reinhard. *Wandlungen unseres Schillerbildes.* Leipzig: Liebisch.

Giese, Rudolf. *Politische Haltung und politische Motive im Drama der Klassiker (Goethe, Schiller, Kleist).* Hamburg and Würzburg: Richard Mayer.

Jäger, Erich. "Führer und Gemeinschaft. Eine Betrachtung im Anschluß an Schillers Wallenstein," *Zeitschrift für Deutschkunde* 52: 521–29.

Storz, Gerhard. *Das Drama Friedrich Schillers*. Frankfurt am Main: Societäts-Verlag.

Vowinckel, Hans August. *Schiller — Der Dichter der Geschichte*. Berlin: Junker & Dünnhaupt.

Wiese, Benno von. *Die Dramen Schillers: Politik und Tragödie*. Leipzig: Bibliographisches Institut AG.

1940

Hohenstein, Lily. *Schiller der Kämpfer, der Dichter*. Berlin: Paul Neff.

Petersen, Julius. *Geschichtsdrama und nationaler Mythos: Grenzfragen zur Gegenwartsform des Dramas*. Stuttgart: Metzler.

1941

Buchwald, Reinhard. "*Maria Stuart* und *Die Jungfrau von Orleans:* Die klassische Kunstform als Träger der sittlichen Ideen und der religiösen Symbole," *Zeitschrift für deutsche Bildung* 17: 215–30.

1943

Bartels, Adolf. *Deutsche Dichter*. Leipzig: Haessel.

Fricke, Gerhard. *Vollendung und Aufbruch: Reden und Aufsätze zur deutschen Dichtung*. Berlin: Jünker & Dünnhaupt.

———. *Wege und Wandlungen deutscher Dichtung von Nietzsche bis zur Gegenwart*. Jena and Leipzig: Wilhelm Gronau W. Agricola.

Ibel, Rudolf. *Weltschau der Dichter*. Jena: Diederichs.

1946

Bohner, Theodor. *Friedrich von Schiller*. Berlin: Aufbau.

1957

Fambach, Oscar. *Schiller und sein Kreis in der Kritik ihrer Zeit*. Berlin: Akademie-Verlag.

1959

Dahlke, Günther, ed. *Der Menschheit Würde: Dokumente zum Schiller-Bild der deutschen Arbeiterklasse*. Weimar: Arion.

Storz, Gerhard. *Der Dichter Friedrich Schiller*. Stuttgart: Klett.

1960

Abusch, Alexander. *Schillers Menschenbild und der sozialistische Humanismus*. Berlin: Aufbau.

Braemer, Edith, and Ursula Wertheim. *Studien zur deutschen Klassik*. Berlin: Rütten & Loening.

1961

Hettner, Hermann. *Geschichte der deutschen Literatur im achtzehnten Jahrhundert*, vol. 2. Berlin: Aufbau.

Korff, Hermann August. *Lessing, Kleist, Schiller, Shaw, Anouilh: Drei Vorträge*. Hanau bei Frankfurt am Main: Werner Dausien.

1962

Hegel, Georg Wilhelm Friedrich. *Hegel on Tragedy*, ed. with an introduction by Anne and Henry Paolucci. New York, Evanston, San Francisco, and London: Harper & Row.

1964

Fontane, Theodor. *Sämtliche Werke*, vol. 22: 1–2. Munich: Nymphenburg.

1965

Abusch, Alexander. *Schiller: Größe und Tragik eines deutschen Genius*. Berlin and Weimar: Aufbau.

1970

Goethe, Johann Wolfgang von. *Kunsthistorische Schriften und Übersetzungen*. Berlin: Aufbau.

Oellers, Norbert, ed. *Schiller — Zeitgenosse aller Epochen: Dokumente zur Wirkungsgeschichte Schillers in Deutschland*, vol. I: *1782–1859*. Frankfurt am Main: Athenäum.

1971

Mueller-Seidel, Walter. "Die Idee des neuen Lebens: Eine Betrachtung über Schillers *Wallenstein*," in P. F. Ganz, ed. *The Discontinuous Tradition: Studies in German Literature in Honour of Ernest Ludwig Stahl*. Oxford: Clarendon.

1973

Ehrig, Heinz. *Paradoxe und absurde Dichtung: Über die Formproblematik von "Geschichte" und "Held" dargestellt in Textbeispielen von Schiller, Kleist und Beckett*. Munich: Fink.

1974

Kraft, Herbert. *Das Schicksalsdrama: Interpretation und Kritik einer literarischen Reihe*. Tübingen: Niemeyer.

1976

Hart-Nibbrig, Christiaan L. "'Die Weltgeschichte ist das Weltgericht': Zur Aktualität von Schillers ästhetischer Geschichtsdeutung," *Jahrbuch der Deutschen Schillergesellschaft* 20: 255–77.

Mueller-Seidel, Walter. "Episches im Theater der deutschen Klassik. Eine Betrachtung über Schillers *Wallenstein*," *Jahrbuch der Deutschen Schillergesellschaft* 20: 338–86.

Oellers, Norbert, ed. *Schiller — Zeitgenosse aller Epochen. Dokumente zur Wirkungsgeschichte Schillers in Deutschland*, vol. II: *1860–1966*. Munich: Beck.

1977

Heuer, Fritz, and Werner Keller, eds. *Schillers Wallenstein*. Darmstadt: Wissenschaftliche Buchgesellschaft.

1979

Hinderer, Walter. *Schillers Dramen: Neue Interpretationen*. Stuttgart: Reclam.

1981

Hinck, Walter, ed. *Geschichte als Schauspiel: Deutsche Geschichtsdramen. Interpretationen*. Frankfurt am Main: Suhrkamp.

1982

Funke, Christoph. *Schillers "Wallenstein," Regie Solter, Deutsche Theater*. Berlin: Henschelverlag.

1989

Albert, Claudia. *Friedrich von Schiller: "Die Jungfrau von Orleans."* Frankfurt am Main: Diesterweg.

Koopmann, Helmut. "Die Tragödie der verhinderten Selbstbestimmung: Schillers Aufklärungsdenken, die französische Revolution und *Wallenstein* als politische Antwort," in Koopmann, ed. *Freiheitssonne und Revolutionsgewitter: Reflexe der Französischen Revolution im literarischen Deutschland zwischen 1789 und 1840*. Tübingen: Niemeyer.

1994

Guthke, Karl. *Schillers Dramen: Idealismus und Skepsis*. Tübingen: Francke.

1995

Dann, Otto, Norbert Oellers, and Ernst Osterkamp, eds. *Schiller als Historiker*. Stuttgart and Weimar: Metzler.

Jäger, Manfred. *Kultur und Politik in der DDR 1945–1990*. Cologne: Edition Deutschland Archiv.

1998

Koopmann, Helmut, ed. *Schiller-Handbuch*. Stuttgart: Körner.

Secondary Sources:

1836

Raumer, Friedrich. *Königinnen Elisabeth und Maria Stuart: Nach den Quellen im britischen Museum und Reichsarchive.* Leipzig: Brockhaus.

1837

Hinrichs, H. F. W. *Schillers Dichtungen nach ihren historischen Beziehungen und nach ihrem inneren Zusammenhänge.* Leipzig: J. C. Hinrichs.

1886

Acton, Lord. "German Schools of History," *English Historical Review* 1: 7–42.

1890

Fester, Richard. *Rousseau und die deutsche Geschichtsphilosophie.* Stuttgart: G. H. Meyer.

1905

Ludwig, Albert. *Das Urteil über Schiller im neunzehnten Jahrhundert: Eine Revision seines Prozesses.* Bonn: Friedrich Cohen.

1910

Kueffner, Louise Mallinckrodt. *The Development of the Historic Drama: Its Theory and Practice. A Study Based Chiefly on the Dramas of Elizabethan England and of Germany.* Chicago: U of Chicago P.

1935

Smith, Herbert. "Present Day Tendencies in the Interpretation of Schiller," *Publications of the English Goethe-Society,* new series 11: 20–36.

1941

Atkins, Henry Gibson. *German Literature through Nazi Eyes.* London: Methuen.

1946

Collingwood, R. G. *The Idea of History.* Oxford: Clarendon.

1952

Mannheim, Karl. *Essays on the Sociology of Knowledge,* ed. Paul Kecskemeti. New York: Oxford UP.

1954

Thyssen, Johannes. *Geschichte der Geschichtsphilosophie.* Bonn: Bouvier.

1955

Wiese, Benno von. *Die deutsche Tragödie von Lessing bis Hebbel,* third ed. Hamburg: Hoffmann & Campe.

1959

Gardiner, Patrick. *Theories of History*. New York: Free Press.

Gilde, Luise. *Friedrich von Schillers Geschichtsphilosophie: Veranschaulicht an seinen Dramen*. London: Gilde.

1961

Steiner, George. *The Death of Tragedy*. New York: Knopf.

1964

Freeden, Herbert. *Jüdisches Theater in Nazideutschland*. Tübingen: Mohr.

Kraus, Karl. *Werke*, ed. Heinrich Fischer. Munich and Vienna: Langen.

1965

Wellek, René. *A History of Modern Criticism: 1750–1950. The Age of Transition*. New Haven and London: Yale UP.

1966

Nolte, Ernst. *Three Faces of Fascism: Action Française, Italian Fascism, National Socialism*, transl. Leila Vennewitz. New York, Chicago, and San Francisco: Holt, Rinehart & Winston.

1967

Brecht, Bertolt. *Gesammelte Werke*. 20 vols. Frankfurt am Main: Suhrkamp.

Demetz, Peter. *Marx, Engels and the Poets: Origins of Marxist Literary Criticism*, transl. Jeffrey L. Sammons. Chicago and London: U of Chicago P.

Kollektiv für Literaturgeschichte. *Johannes R. Becher*, ed. Horst Gorsch. Berlin: Volk und Wissen.

Staiger, Emil. *Schiller*. Zurich: Atlantis.

Werner, Karl Ferdinand. *Das NS-Geschichtsbild und die deutsche Geschichtswissenschaft*. Stuttgart, Berlin, Cologne, and Mainz: Kohlhammer.

1968

Burschell, Friedrich. *Schiller*. Reinbek bei Hamburg: Rowohlt.

1969

Sengle, Friedrich. *Das historische Drama in Deutschland: Geschichte eines literarischen Mythos*. Stuttgart: Metzler.

Solger, Karl Wilhelm. *Vorlesungen über Aesthetik*. Darmstadt: Wissenschaftliche Buchgesellschaft.

1970

Fischer, David Hackett. *Historian's Fallacies: Toward a Logic of Historical Thought.* New York, Evanston IL, and London: Harper & Row.

Lecke, Bodo, ed. *Dichter über ihre Dichtungen: Friedrich Schiller von 1795–1805.* Munich: Heimeran.

1971

Gilman, Sander, ed. *Nationalsozialistische Literaturtheorie: Eine Dokumentation.* Frankfurt am Main: Athenäum.

Haider-Pregler, Hilde. "Das Dritte Reich und das Theater," *Maske und Kothurn* 17: 203–14.

Heller, Erich, *The Disinherited Mind: Essays in Modern German Literature and Thought*, third ed. New York: Barnes & Noble.

1974

Paul, Ulrike. *Vom Geschichtsdrama zur politischen Diskussion: Über die Desintegration von Individuum und Geschichte bei Georg Büchner und Peter Weiss.* Munich: Fink.

1975

Berghahn, Klaus, ed. *Friedrich Schiller: Zur Geschichtlichkeit seines Werkes.* Kronberg (Ts.): Scriptor.

Blumensath, Heinz, and Christel Uebach. *Einführung in die Literaturgeschichte der DDR.* Stuttgart: Metzler.

Lindenberger, Herbert. *Historical Drama: The Relation of Literature and Reality.* Chicago and London: U of Chicago P.

Reill, Peter Hanns. *The German Enlightenment and the Rise of Historicism.* Berkeley: U of California P.

1976

Berlin, Isaiah. *Vico and Herder: Two Studies in the History of Ideas.* New York: Viking.

Camigliano, Albert J. *Friedrich Schiller und Christian Gottfried Körner: A Critical Relationship.* Stuttgart: Akademischer Verlag Heinz.

Denkler, Horst, and Karl Prümm, eds. *Die deutsche Literatur im Dritten Reich: Themen, Traditionen, Wirkungen.* Stuttgart: Reclam.

1977

Sammons, Jeffrey L. *Literary Sociology and Practical Criticism: An Inquiry.* Bloomington and London: Indiana UP.

Steck, Paul. *Schiller und Shakespeare: Idee und Wirklichkeit*. Frankfurt am Main, Bern, and Las Vegas: Peter Lang.

1978

Hoy, David Couzens. *The Critical Circle: Literature, History and Philosophical Hermeneutics*. Berkeley, Los Angeles, and London: U of California P.

1979

Ruppelt, Georg. *Schiller im nationalsozialistischen Deutschland*. Stuttgart: Metzler.

Schlegel, Friedrich von. *Kritische Ausgabe seiner Werke*, ed. Ernst Behler, vol. 18. Munich and Zurich: Schöningh.

1980

Neubuhr, Elfriede, ed. *Geschichtsdrama*. Darmstadt: Wissenschaftliche Buchgesellschaft.

1981

Jameson, Fredric. *The Political Unconscious: Narrative as a Socially Symbolic Act*. Ithaca NY: Cornell UP.

Pillau, Helmut. *Die fortgedachte Dissonanz: Hegels Tragödientheorie und Schillers Tragödie. Deutsche Antworten auf die Französische Revolution*. Munich: Fink.

1982

Sammons, Jeffrey L. Review of *Schiller im nationalsozialistischen Deutschland: Der Versuch einer Gleichschaltung*, by Georg Ruppelt, *German Quarterly* 55: 127–28.

1983

"*Das war ein Vorspiel nur . . .*": *Bücherverbrennung Deutschland 1933. Voraussetzungen und Folgen*. Ausstellung der Akademie der Künste vom 8. Mai bis 3. Juli 1983. Berlin: Medusa.

Iggers, Georg G. *The German Conception of History: The National Tradition of Historical Thought from Herder to the Present*. Middletown CT: Wesleyan UP.

1984

De Man, Paul. *The Rhetoric of Romanticism*. New York: Columbia UP.

1985

Lessing, Gotthold Ephraim. *Werke*, vol. 6: *1767–1769*. Frankfurt am Main: Deutsche Klassiker.

1986

Wikander, Matthew H. *The Play of Truth and State: Historical Drama from Shakespeare to Brecht*. Baltimore: Johns Hopkins UP.

1987

Ueding, Gert. *Klassik und Romantik: Deutsche Literatur im Zeitalter der Französischen Revolution 1789–1815*. Munich and Vienna: Hanser.

White, Hayden. *The Content of the Form: Narrative Discourse and Historical Representation*. Baltimore and London: Johns Hopkins UP.

1988

Hohendahl, Peter Uwe, ed. *A History of German Literary Criticism, 1730–1980*, with contributions by Klaus L. Berghahn, Russell A. Berman, Peter Uwe Hohendahl, Jochen Schulte-Sasse, and Bernhard Zimmermann, transl. Franz Blaha, John R. Blazek, Jeffrey S. Librett, and Simon Srebrny. Lincoln and London: U of Nebraska P.

Jonas, Gisela, ed. *Schiller-Debatte 1905: Dokumente zur Literaturtheorie und Literaturkritiker revolutionären deutschen Sozialdemokratie*. Berlin: Akademie-Verlag.

1989

Grumley, John E. *History and Totality: Radical Historicism from Hegel to Foucault*. London and New York: Routledge.

Thomas, Brook. *The New Historicism and Other Old-Fashioned Topics*. Princeton: Princeton UP.

1990

Eggert, Hartmut, Ulrich Profitlich, and Klaus R. Scherpe, eds. *Geschichte als Literatur: Formen und Grenzen der Repräsentation von Vergangenheit*. Stuttgart: Metzler.

Iggers, Georg G., and James M. Powell *Leopold von Ranke and the Shaping of the Historical Discipline*. Syracuse NY: Syracuse UP.

1991

Jameson, Fredric. *Postmodernism; or, The Cultural Logic of Late Capitalism*. Durham NC: Duke UP.

Reed, T. J. *Schiller*. Oxford and New York: Oxford UP.

1994

Albert, Claudia. *Deutsche Klassiker im Nationalsozialismus: Schiller, Kleist, Hölderlin*. Stuttgart: Metzler.

Bedarida, François, ed. *The Social Responsibility of the Historian*. Providence RI and Oxford: Berghahn.

Bernstein, Michael André. *Foregone Conclusions: Against Apocalyptic History*. Berkeley: U of California P.

Hammer, Stephanie Barbé. "Schiller, Time and Again," *German Quarterly* 67, no. 2: 153–72.

Hermand, Jost. *Geschichte der Germanistik*. Reinbek bei Hamburg: Rowohlt.

1995

Bambach, Charles R. *Heidegger, Dilthey and the Crisis of Historicism*. Ithaca and London: Cornell UP.

Behler, Constantin. *Nostalgic Teleology: Friedrich Schiller and the Schemata of Aesthetic Humanism*. New York, Bern, and Frankfurt am Main: Peter Lang.

1996

Fulda, Daniel. *Wissenschaft aus Kunst: Die Entstehung der modernen Geschichtsschreibung 1760–1860*. Berlin and New York: De Gruyter.

Hamilton, Paul. *Historicism*. London and New York: Routledge.

Knobloch, Hans-Jörg, and Helmut Koopmann, eds. *Schiller heute*. Tübingen: Stauffenburg.

1997

Bohn, Thomas M. Review of *Wissenschaft aus Kunst: Die Entstehung der modernen Geschichtsschreibung 1760–1860*, by Daniel Fulda, *Comparativ* 7, no. 4: 112–13.

Evans, Richard J. *In Defence of History*. London: Granta.

Index

Abusch, Alexander, 112, 113, 119, 120–21, 122, 123, 124–25, 127, 131, 132, 154, 155
Ackerman, Anton, 115–16
Acton, Lord, 44, 64, 157
Albert, Claudia, 87, 106, 139, 145, 149, 156, 161
Alexander, G. G. (Gertrud) L., 112, 114
American Revolution, 123
Apel, Johann, 28
Aristotle, 3, 10, 142, 145
astrology, 6, 17, 21, 41, 76, 79, 80, 83, 103, 114, 121, 123, 136, 137
Atkins, Henry Gibson, 157

Bambach, Charles R., 162
Baroque drama, 4
Bartels, Adolf, 106, 154
Baumgarten, Heinrich, 45
Becher, Johannes R., 1, 12, 115, 135, 158
Bedarida, François, 9, 12, 161
Behler, Constantin, 162
Bellermann, Ludwig, 152
Berger, Karl, 152
Berghahn, Klaus, 8, 32, 159, 161
Berlin, Isaiah, 159
Berman, Russell, 87, 132, 161
Bernstein, Michael André, 139, 149, 162
Bible, 4, 18–19, 70
Bitterfelder Weg, 117
Bloch, Ernst, 119

Blumensath, Heinz, 110, 111, 114, 115, 118, 132, 159
Bohn, Thomas M., 149, 162
Bohner, Theodor, 154
Bonaparte, Napoleon, 45, 46–47, 82, 121, 143
Borcherdt, Hans Heinrich, 85–86, 87, 103, 153
Böttiger, Karl August, 18–19, 58, 60
Braemer, Edith, 119, 122–24, 125, 126–32, 154
Braig-München, Friedrich, 103–4, 106, 153
Brandes, Ernst, 28
Braun, Julius, 20, 22, 23, 25, 29, 31, 32, 152
Brecht, Bertolt, 5, 72, 115, 117, 132, 136, 158
Büchner, Georg, 5, 35, 38
Büchner, Georg, works by: *Woyzeck*, 35
Buchwald, Reinhard, 104–5, 106, 153, 154
Bulthaupt, Heinrich, 57–58, 64, 152
Burschell, Friedrich, 158

Camigliano, Albert J., 159
catharsis, 2
Catholicism, 26, 35, 41, 98, 103, 113
Chamberlain, Houston Stewart, 91
Church, 13, 39, 49, 55
Collingwood, R. G., 157

Cysarz, Herbert, 95–96, 106, 153

Dahlke, Günther, 110, 112–13, 114, 132, 154
Dann, Otto, 150, 156
Darwin, Charles, 91
De Man, Paul, 2, 12, 160
Demetz, Peter, 132, 158
Denkler, Horst, 106, 159
Deubel, Werner, 94, 96, 106, 153
Dilthey, Wilhelm, 8, 45, 67, 68, 70–78, 87, 104, 147, 153
Dostoevsky, Fyodor, 67
Dumouriez, Charles, 18, 120, 140, 143
Düntzer, Heinrich, 59–63, 64, 151, 152

Eder, Jürgen, 137, 138, 149
Eggert, Hartmut, 161
Ehrig, Heinz, 155
Eichendorff, Josef Freiherr von, 36
Elm, Theo, 147–48, 149
Engels, Friedrich, 110, 112, 120
Enlightenment, the, 3, 4, 13, 14, 24, 26, 27, 28, 31, 32, 34, 44, 48, 91, 103, 122, 129, 138, 159
Evans, Richard J., 138, 149, 162

Fabricius, Hans, 87, 102, 103, 106, 153
Fambach, Oscar, 19, 32, 154
Fessler and Rhode, 22, 25, 26
Fester, Richard, 157
Fichte, Johann Gottlieb, 14
First World War, 3, 5, 63, 67–69, 70, 81, 83–84, 135

Fischer, David Hackett, 149, 158
Fontane, Theodor, 55–56, 64, 155
Freeden, Herbert, 105, 106, 158
French Revolution, 51, 95, 109, 110, 120, 123, 126, 127, 129, 130, 131, 141–42, 145, 148
Freud, Sigmund, 67, 70
Freytag, Gustav, 47–48
Fricke, Gerhard, 93, 100–101, 102, 103, 106, 107, 153, 154
Fulda, Daniel, 138, 149, 162
Funke, Christoph, 135, 149, 156

Gardiner, Patrick, 70, 87, 158
Gerhard, Ute, 38, 63
Giese, Rudolf, 101–2, 107, 153
Gilde, Luise, 158
Gilman, Sander, 91, 92, 93, 94, 107, 159
Glück, Alfons, 142, 143
Gobineau, Joseph Artur de, 91
God, 13, 43, 51, 54, 104
Goebbels, Joseph, 90, 94
Goethe, Johann Wolfgang von, 1, 3, 8, 12, 15, 16–18, 19, 22, 32, 34, 37, 38, 42, 48, 57, 64, 74, 87, 88, 91, 94, 99, 100, 118, 120, 121, 126, 140, 143, 144, 155
Goethe, Johann Wolfgang von, works by: *Egmont,* 5, 16, 24, 42, 74; *Götz von Berlichingen,* 16, 24, 123
Gottsched, Johann Christoph, 3
Grabbe, Christian Dietrich, 5, 24, 38
Greek tragedy, 2, 19, 120, 142
Grillparzer, Franz, 24

Grimm, Jacob, 91
Grotewohl, Otto, 116
Grumley, John E., 87, 161
Gryphius, Andreas, 4
Guthke, Karl, 145–47, 149, 156

Haider-Pregler, Hilde, 93, 107, 159
Hamilton, Paul, 162
Hammer, Stephanie Barbé, 142, 149, 162
Hart-Nibbrig, Christiaan L., 136–37, 149, 155
Harth, Dietrich, 138
Haupt- und Staatsaktionen, 4
Hebbel, Christian Friedrich, 48
Hegel, Georg Wilhelm Friedrich, 19, 33, 34–35, 44, 48, 55, 64, 78, 148, 155
Heller, Erich, 69, 88, 159
Herder, Johann Gottfried, 8, 19, 21, 33–34, 45, 51, 68, 69, 70, 87, 91, 152, 159, 160
Hermand, Jost, 9, 122, 132, 148, 150, 162
Herwegh, Georg, 38
Hettner, Hermann, 48–49, 64, 155
Heuer, Fritz, 32, 156
Hinck, Walter, 12, 150, 156
Hinderer, Walter, 137, 150, 156
Hinrichs, H. F., 40, 64, 157
historical inaccuracies, 6, 17, 19, 24, 25, 26, 27, 31, 37, 39–40, 41, 42, 44, 47, 48, 53, 60, 61, 62, 78, 80, 84, 86, 87, 96, 98, 99, 104, 106, 121, 124, 127, 128, 130, 147
Hitler, Adolf, 5, 82, 87, 89, 90, 92, 93, 102, 114, 115, 153
Hoffmeister, Karl, 36, 38–44, 52, 62, 64, 141, 151

Hohendahl, Peter Uwe, 8, 12, 32, 65, 87, 132, 161
Hohenstein, Lily, 98, 103, 107, 154
Die Horen, 15, 92
Hoy, David Couzens, 160
Humboldt, Wilhelm von, 33, 34, 45

Ibel, Rudolf, 107, 154
Iggers, Georg G., 33, 35, 45, 46, 64, 88, 160, 161

Jagemann, Caroline, 126
Jäger, Erich, 101, 107, 153
Jäger, Manfred, 115, 116, 117, 132, 156
Jameson, Fredric, 160, 161
Johnston, Otto, 7, 12, 140–41, 144, 146, 150
Jonas, Gisela, 161

Kant, Immanuel, 7, 14, 67, 68, 69, 94, 101, 110
Keller, Werner, 32, 156
Kepler, Johannes, 76
Khevenhüller, Franz Christophs von, 56
Klages, Ludwig, 94, 96
Klopstock, Friedrich Gottlieb, 87
Knobloch, Hans-Jörg, 149, 162
Kommerell, Max, 87, 88, 152
Koopmann, Helmut, 12, 63, 64, 87, 88, 123, 132, 137, 138, 139, 141, 142, 146, 149, 150, 156, 162
Korff, Hermann August, 82–85, 88, 152, 155
Körner, Christian Gottfried, 9, 123, 159
Kraft, Herbert, 143, 150, 155
Kraus, Karl, 1, 12, 158

Kueffner, Louise Mallinckrodt, 157
Kühne, Ferdinand Gustav, 46–47

Lamport, Francis John, 145
Lecke, Bodo, 32, 159
Lenin, Vladimir Ilyich, 110, 111, 114, 115, 116, 135
Lessing, Gotthold Ephraim, 3, 4, 16, 17, 18, 19, 20, 21, 25, 31, 35, 46, 59, 73, 99, 118
Lessing, Gotthold Ephraim, works by: *Hamburgische Dramaturgie*, 4, 17, 24, 32, 160
Linden, Walter, 96–97, 107, 153
Lindenberger, Herbert, 159
Ludwig, Albert, 32, 36, 38, 64, 88, 157
Ludwig, Otto, 47, 83, 152
Lukács, Georg, 119
Luxemburg, Rosa, 112

Mannheim, Karl, 69, 86, 88, 157
Marx, Karl, 110, 112, 120
marxism, 45, 50, 89, 93, 109–11, 114, 115, 122, 124, 127, 131, 135, 136, 141
Mayer, Hans, 119
Mehnert, Günter, 111
Mehring, Franz, 112–13, 124, 125, 126
Meinecke, Friedrich, 46
Merkel, Garlieb, 21, 24, 26, 29–30
Merkur, 7
Meyer, Heinrich, 17, 120
Michel, Markus, 135

Middle Ages, 13, 27, 43, 49, 50, 62, 81, 91, 95, 103, 141, 146
miracles, 28, 29, 30, 43, 129
Mueller-Seidel, Walter, 136, 150, 155, 156
Muhlack, Ulrich, 138

nationalism, 3, 15, 33, 36, 37, 47, 91, 97, 119, 120, 123, 125, 129, 130, 147
nature, 3, 22, 48, 76–77, 79, 81, 144
Neubuhr, Elfriede, 160
New Historicism, 4, 5, 8, 10, 11, 13, 27, 74, 137, 138, 148
Nibelungenlied, 98
Niebuhr, Barthold Georg, 44
Nietzsche, Friedrich, 8, 9, 67, 70, 81
Nolte, Ernst, 89, 107, 158

Oellers, Norbert, 32, 47, 64, 88, 150, 155, 156
Old Norse sagas, 92
Osterkamp, Ernst, 150, 156

Paul, Ulrike, 159
Paur, Theodor, 56
Peasants' War, 123
Petersen, Julius, 97–100, 107, 153, 154
Piccolomini, E., 56
Pillau, Helmut, 160
Plutarch, 74
Pongs, Hermann, 102, 107, 153
Powell, James M., 45, 64, 161
postmodern, 2, 5, 8, 11, 137, 139, 147, 148
Preußische Jahrbücher (Prussian Yearbooks), 45
Profitlich, Ulrich, 161

Prümm, Karl, 106, 159

Raff, Helene, 56–57, 65, 153
Ranke, Leopold von, 8, 31, 33, 34, 46, 44–46, 56, 59, 64, 70, 77, 78, 80, 91, 138, 161
Raumer, Friedrich, 39–40, 65, 157
Reed, T. J., 161
Reill, Peter Hanns, 13, 32, 159
Reinhardt, Hartmut, 142–44, 150
Rickert, Heinrich, 67, 68
Robertson, William, 26
Romanticism, 12, 15, 26, 34, 37, 38, 44, 50, 65, 71, 160
Rönnefahrt, J. G., 49–55, 65, 151, 152
Rosenberg, Alfred, 90
Die rote Fahne, 113–14
Ruppelt, Georg, 90, 91, 94, 105, 107, 160
Rüsen, Jörn, 138

Sammons, Jeffrey L., 132, 158, 159, 160
Sautermeister, Gert, 145, 150
Schelling, Friedrich Wilhelm Joseph von, 14
Scherpe, Klaus R., 161
Schiller, Johann Friedrich von, other works by:
  "Der Antritt des neuen Jahrhunderts" ("The Beginning of a New Century"), 62
  Die ästhetische Erziehung des Menschen in einer Reihe von Briefen (The Aesthetic Education of Man in a Series of Letters), 2, 7
  Die Braut von Messina (The Bride of Messina), 2, 77
  Demetrius, 77
  Dom Karlos Infant von Spanien (Don Carlos Infant of Spain), 6, 28, 40, 103, 147
  Geschichte des Abfalles der Niederlande (History of the Defeat of the Netherlands), 8, 28, 85
  Geschichte des Dreßigjährigen Kriegs (History of the Thirty Years' War), 8, 16, 38, 58, 75, 79, 82, 85, 148
  "Die Glocke," 1
  Die Räuber (The Robbers), 15, 59, 109, 110
  "Die Schaubühne als eine moralische Anstalt betrachtet" ("The Stage Seen as a Moral Institution"), 7, 93
  "Über das Erhabene" ("On the Sublime"), 102, 143
  "Über das Pathetische" ("On Pathos"), 2, 26
  "Über die tragische Kunst" ("On Tragedy"), 2, 3
  Über naïve und sentimentalische Dichtung (On Naïve and Sentimental Poetry), 2
  "Über Völkerwanderung, Kreuzzüge und Mittelalter" ("About Mass Migration, Crusades and the Middle Ages"), 27
  Die Verschwörung des Fiesko zu Genua (The Conspiracy of Fiesco at Genoa), 6
  Wilhelm Tell, 73, 77, 105, 118
Schlegel, Friedrich, 10, 12, 15, 160
Schlegel, Wilhelm, 15, 43

Schleiermacher, Friedrich, 33
Schlözer, August Ludwig von, 7, 14, 70, 89
Schulte-Sasse, Jochen, 65, 161
Schulz, Gerhard, 140, 144–45, 150
science, 5, 8, 13, 45, 68, 69, 70, 73, 86, 93, 96, 113, 115, 138
scientific (approach, method, view), 5, 8, 13, 31, 34, 45, 46, 60, 67, 69, 70, 71, 78, 81, 84, 91, 92, 137
Second World War, 102, 114, 135
Seghers, Anna, 117
Sengle, Friedrich, 12, 16–17, 32, 158
Shakespeare, William, 4, 25, 29, 35, 36, 37, 38, 42, 43, 49, 57, 61, 71, 73, 74, 76, 77, 81, 84, 98
Sharpe, Lesley, 146
Shaw, George Bernard, 146
Smith, Herbert, 100, 107, 157
Solger, Karl Wilhelm, 43, 65, 158
Spengler, Oswald, 8, 68–69, 71, 82, 85, 86
Spengler, Wilhelm, 104
Staiger, Emil, 142, 158
Stalin, Joseph, 111, 114, 115, 117
Steck, Paul, 159
Steiner, George, 7, 12, 35, 65, 158
Storz, Gerhard, 108, 144, 150, 154
Strich, Fritz, 78–81, 88, 152
Stuckert, Franz, 105, 108, 153
Sturm und Drang [Storm and Stress], 5, 15
Süvern, W., 19, 151
Sybel, Heinrich, 45

Thalheim, Hans-Günther, 119
Thirty Years' War, 6, 8, 18, 37, 55, 57, 76, 119, 120–21, 122, 144
Thomas, Brook, 161
Thyssen, Johannes, 157
Tieck, Ludwig, 36–37, 38, 44, 65, 151
Tomaschek, Karl, 58–59, 65, 152
Treitschke, Heinrich, 45

Uebach, Christel, 110, 111, 114, 115, 132, 159
Ueberweg, Friedrich, 65, 152
Ueding, Gert, 35, 65, 161
universal history, 8, 13–14, 15, 33, 35, 44, 45, 70
Universalgeschichte, 8, 13–14, 15, 24, 31, 33, 70, 78, 89, 104

Vierhaus, Rudolf, 46
Voltaire, 43, 81, 113, 141
Vowinckel, Hans August, 108, 154

Wanderscheck, Hermann, 92, 94
Weber, Max, 70
Weber, Wolfgang, 138
Weimar Republic, 3, 68, 71, 81, 93, 113
Wellek, René, 48, 65, 88, 133, 158
Werner, Karl Ferdinand, 91, 92, 108, 158
Wertheim, Ursula, 119, 122–24, 130, 132, 154
Weyhe-Eimke, Freiherr Arnold von, 56
White, Hayden, 10, 137, 138, 148, 161

Wiese, Benno von, 93, 101,
  106, 108, 122, 142, 150,
  154, 157
Wikander, Matthew, 160
Winckelmann, Johann Joachim,
  59
Windelband, Wilhelm, 67–68
wonders, 27, 30, 41, 50, 58,
  105, 129
World War, *see* First World War;
  Second World War

Zetkin, Klara, 112

OHIO UNIVERSITY LIBRARY

Please return this book as soon as you have finished with it. In order to avoid a fine it must be returned by the latest date stamped below. All books are subject to recall after two weeks or immediately if needed for reserve.

MAR 0 1 2005

MAR 2 5 2005

MAR 0 8 2005

CF